Macmillan Natural and Social SCIENCE

Primary 3 Pupil's Book

Pupils are reminded that they should not write in this book.

Helen Sanderson

Course consultant: Rocío Gutiérrez Burgos

Science consultant: Graham Peacock

MACMILLAN

Contents

	Content		Let's investigate!
Unit 7 **Water and air on Earth**	• Where we find water • Characteristics of air • Wind • Weather • Freshwater	• The water cycle • Reading: The drought • Writing: How I use and save water	• Does air have weight? • What's the wind speed, rainfall and temperature where you are?
Unit 8 **Landscapes**	• Different landscapes • Mountain landscapes • Flat landscapes • Relief maps • Rivers	• Coastal landscapes • Coastal landscapes change • Protecting coastal landscapes • Reading: A trip down the river • Writing: My local area	• Can you make a relief map?
Unit 5–8 **Review**	• Science Club Quiz • Science Challenge		
Unit 9 **The top layer of Earth**	• Soil • Soil layers • Types of soil • The soil ecosystem	• Rocks and minerals • Reading: An amazing discovery • Writing: The soil where I live	• How do soil layers form?
Unit 10 **Transport and communication**	• Transport • Land transport • Air and sea transport • Private and public transport • Personal communication • Mass communication	• Computers and the internet • Advertisements • Reading: The Science Club blog • Writing: My transport for the future	• What's the most common form of transport in your class? • Do advertisements work?
Unit 11 **Work**	• The three job sectors • Primary sector: Arable farming • Primary sector: Livestock farming • Natural resources from the sea • Natural resources from the Earth	• Secondary sector: Craft and industry • Tertiary sector: Providing a service • Reading: The Science Club volunteers • Writing: A job description	• Which job sector do most of your classmates' families work in?
Unit12 **Where we live**	• Places • Places change • Services in a city • Maps • Reading: Lost! • Writing: Where I live		• How can you help people find places in your school?
Unit 9–12 **Review**	• Science Club Quiz • Science Challenge		

Welcome to the Science Club

Welcome to the Science Club!
Hello, I'm Clara. I'm a member of the Science Club, too! I'm interested in the Earth and the places where we live.

1 Living things — Identifying living things

In this unit we're going to learn about living things. What living things and non-living things can you see in the picture?

In our world there are **living things** and **non-living things**. **People**, **animals** and **plants** are living things. You are a living thing!

All living things have the same characteristics. They are **born**, they **grow**, they **reproduce** and they **die**. Living things need **food**, **water** and **air** to live.

Some non-living things are **natural**, which means that people don't make them. Water, air and rocks are natural non-living things.

Other non-living things are **man-made**, which means that people make them. Cars, buildings and clothes are man-made non-living things.

DID YOU KNOW?

The Galapagos tortoise is the longest-living animal in the world. It can live for about 150 years!

1 **Copy the charts and identify living things and non-living things in the picture.**

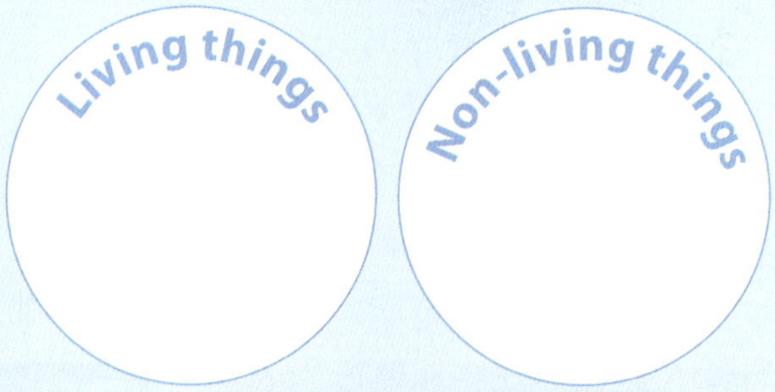

2 **Listen to Clara and Nico talking about living things and non-living things.**

3 **What living things and non-living things do you see on your way to school?**

4 **What are the characteristics of living things?**

5 **Copy and complete the charts.**

Natural non-living things

Man-made non-living things

Life processes of living things

CD1 8

All living things have three life processes: **nutrition**, **interaction** and **reproduction**.

Nutrition

All living things need food for energy and to grow. People and animals eat plants or other animals. Plants use sunlight to make their own food.

Interaction

All living things interact. Moving, touching and communicating are some forms of interaction.

Reproduction

All living things reproduce. Reproduction means making new living things.

a

b

c

1 CD1 7 **Say the *Life processes* chant.**

2 **Identify the three life processes in photos a, b and c.**

3 **Copy and complete the sentence about living things.**

interaction   reproduction   nutrition

All living things have three life processes:  ,  and  .

4 CD1 9 **Say the *Life processes* rap.**

Life processes: People

CD1 10

Like all living things, **people** have three life processes.

- **Nutrition**: We need to eat a **balanced diet** and have **regular meals** to give us energy to grow, work and play.
- **Interaction**: We have contact with other people every day. We can talk to each other and we can show and say how we feel. Many people live in families and love, help and respect each other.
- **Reproduction**: People reproduce and have babies. A mother usually has one baby at a time, but sometimes she can have two or more!

a

b

c

1 **Identify the three life processes in photos a, b and c.**

2 **Are all families the same?**

3 **Order the letters to find some ways that people interact.**

latk cerstpe alpy pleh kowr

4 **How can you help at home?**

Life processes: Animals

Animals interact with each other, with their surroundings and with people. They walk, swim or fly to find food and shelter. Some animals live in groups for protection, but other animals live alone. Although animals can't speak like people, they can make sounds and use movement to communicate.

shelter *(noun)* a place protected from bad weather and predators.

Animals can't make their own food. Some animals eat other animals, some animals eat plants, and there are some animals that eat both animals and plants. Can you remember how we classify these animals?

Some animals are **born live** while other animals are **born from eggs**. Big animals usually have one or two babies, but small animals can have lots of babies!

DID YOU KNOW?

Clown fish can lay over 500 eggs! The father looks after the baby fish.

1. **Which photos show nutrition, interaction and reproduction?**
2. **Why do you think some animals live in groups?**
3. **Can you remember what we call animals that eat plants, other animals, and plants and other animals?**
4. **Can you think of an animal that usually has more than one baby?**
5. **Sing the *Life processes of animals* song.**

CD1 16

Like people and animals, plants have three life processes: **nutrition**, **interaction** and **reproduction**. Plants use sunlight, water and nutrients in the soil to make their own food. Plants interact with their surroundings, and they reproduce by making seeds that grow into new plants.

Investigate how plants interact.

How do plants interact?

You need:

- a flowering plant

a Put the plant next to a window.

b Turn the plant away from the window.

c Make a prediction.

1 The plant dies.
2 The plant doesn't move.
3 The plant turns towards the Sun.

CD1 17

Although plants don't interact like people and animals, they interact with their environment. In this investigation we can see the plant interacting with the Sun.

1 Which life process do you investigate here?

2 Order and copy the sentences. Complete your observations.

Next, we turned the plant away from the window.

We observed that the plant …

First, we put the plant next to a window.

3 Why does *mimosa pudica* close its leaves when you touch it?

DID YOU KNOW?

Some plants have sensitive leaves. *Mimosa pudica* closes its leaves when we touch it.

The rock pool

Sometimes it's difficult to tell if a living thing is a plant or an animal. The sea anemone looks like a plant, but in fact it's an invertebrate that lives in the sea. Sea anemones are born, they grow, they reproduce and they die. They're carnivores and they eat other small animals by catching them with their tentacles. Sea anemones can move, but they usually stay in the same place. Never touch sea anemones because they are venomous!

MY SCIENCE PROJECT

LIVING AND NON-LIVING THINGS NEAR ME

1 **Take a photo of a place near you.**

2 **Find the living things and non-living things in the photo.**

3 **Write a text about these living things and non-living things.**

4 **How are the living things interacting?**

REMEMBER!

The living things are people.....

This is a photo of me and my friends at a beach near my house. Some of the things in the photo are living things. The living things are people, plants and bushes. Some of the things in the photo are non-living things. The non-living things are houses, sand, the sea and my kite. I love spending time with my friends at the beach!

Learning to learn

1 Copy and complete the word maps.

reproduction   people   natural   plants   nutrition

Living things

- ______

- animals

- ______

Life processes of living things

- ______

- interaction

- ______

Non-living things

- ______

- man-made

2 Use the word maps to copy and complete the sentences.

a Living things can be people, ______ or ______ .

b They have three life processes: ______ , interaction and ______ .

c Non-living things can be natural or ______ .

3 True or false? Copy the sentences and correct the ones that are false.

a Animals and plants are living things.
b Non-living things are born.
c Living things are born, grow, reproduce and die.
d Non-living things can be natural or man-made.

4 Copy the chart and classify the living things and non-living things.

fish building dog bear rock plant car water

Living things	Non-living things

5 Identify the life processes in photos a, b and c.

a

b

c

I know the differences between living and non-living things. ☆ ☆ ☆

I can identify and describe the life processes of living things. ☆ ☆ ☆

I know how plants interact. ☆ ☆ ☆

2 The senses — How we use our senses

In this unit we're going to learn about the senses and the nervous system.

Our senses tell us about the world around us. Look at the picture. What can Clara see, hear, smell, taste and touch?

CD1 21

We use our **senses** and our **nervous system** to interact with the world around us. We have five senses: **sight**, **hearing**, **smell**, **taste** and **touch**. Each of these senses sends a message through the nervous system to our **brain** so we know what is happening around us and can respond.

CD1 23

Our **eyes** are the organs of **sight**. We can see different shapes, sizes and colours.

Our **ears** are the organs of **hearing**. We can hear sounds that are loud and sounds that are quiet.

Our **nose** is the organ of **smell**. We can identify good and bad smells.

Our **tongue** is the organ of **taste**. We can identify different tastes: sweet, salty, bitter and sour.

Our **skin** is the organ of **touch**. We can feel things that are hot or cold, soft or hard and rough or smooth.

1 CD1 20 **Listen to Clara at the fair.**

2 **What are the five senses?**

3 CD1 22 **Say *The five senses* chant.**

4 Me **How do you use your senses every day?**

5 CD1 24 **Say *The five senses* rap.**

6 **Match the organs to the senses. Write sentences.**

a	eyes	hearing
b	ears	smell
c	nose	touch
d	tongue	sight
e	skin	taste

Our eyes are the organs of sight.

We can see

CD1 25

Our **eyes** are the organs of sight. Our eyes are very delicate and are protected by our **eyebrows**, **eyelashes** and **eyelids**. These stop sweat and dust getting into our eyes.

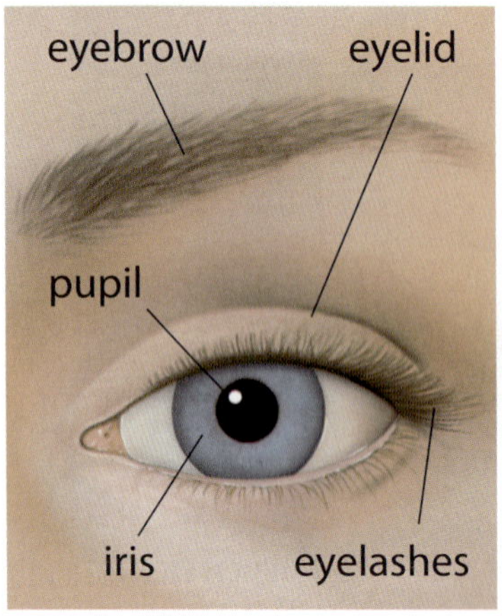

sweat *(noun)* liquid that forms on your skin when you are hot.

CD1 26

The **iris** is a big coloured circle at the front of the eye. The **pupil** is a black circle in the middle of the iris. Light enters the eye through the pupil and it makes an image on the **retina** at the back of the eye. The retina sends this information to our brain, and this is what we see.

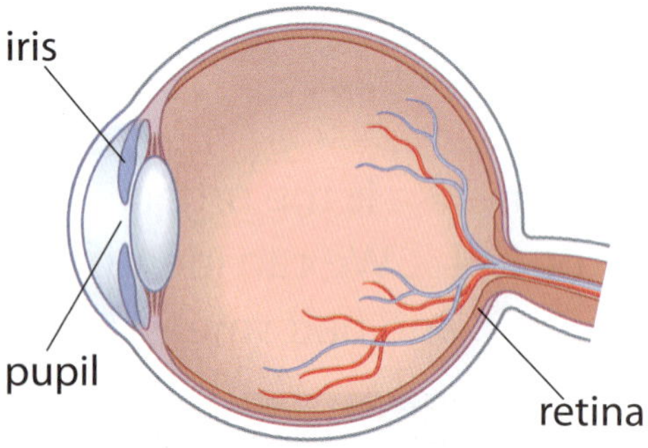

CD1 27

Our eyes are very delicate so we must look after them:

- Visit the optician's regularly.
- Wear glasses if you need them.
- Always read with good light.
- Don't spend too long using a computer.
- Don't sit too near the television.

DID YOU KNOW?

It's impossible to sneeze with our eyes open!

1 **Are these parts of the eye for sight or for protection?**

pupil eyebrows eyelashes iris

2 **What colour irises have your classmates got?**

3 Me **How can you look after your eyes?**

Make a pinhole viewer.

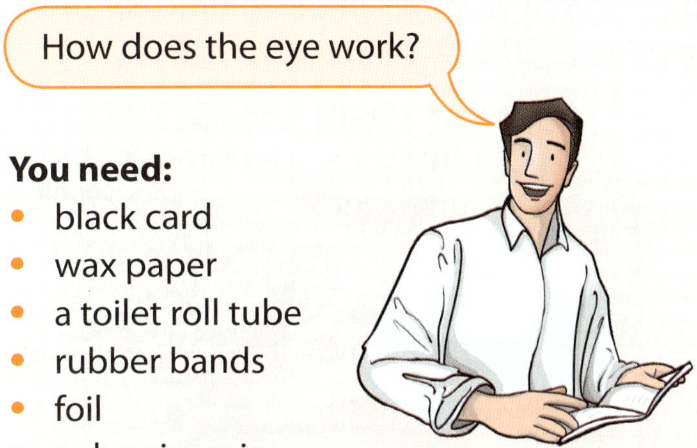

You need:
- black card
- wax paper
- a toilet roll tube
- rubber bands
- foil
- a drawing pin

a

Use a rubber band to cover one end of the toilet roll tube with foil.

b

Use a rubber band to cover the other end of the toilet roll tube with wax paper.

c
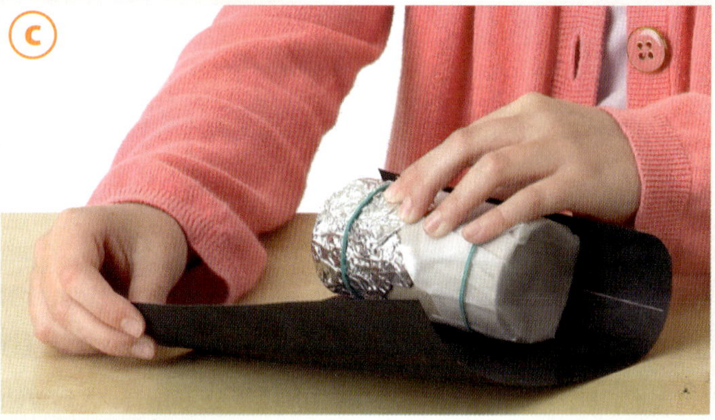
Cover the toilet roll tube with black card.

d

Make a small hole in the foil.

e

Hold the end with the wax paper to your eye. Look through the pinhole viewer.

f Discuss the results.

1 Which part of the pinhole viewer represents the pupil?
2 Which part of the pinhole viewer represents the retina?

We can hear

CD1 29

Our **ears** are the organs of hearing. Our ears have three parts: the **outer ear**, the **middle ear** and the **inner ear**. The outer ear is the part of our ear that is visible. In the middle ear there is the **eardrum** and there are **three small bones**. The **cochlea** is in the inner ear.

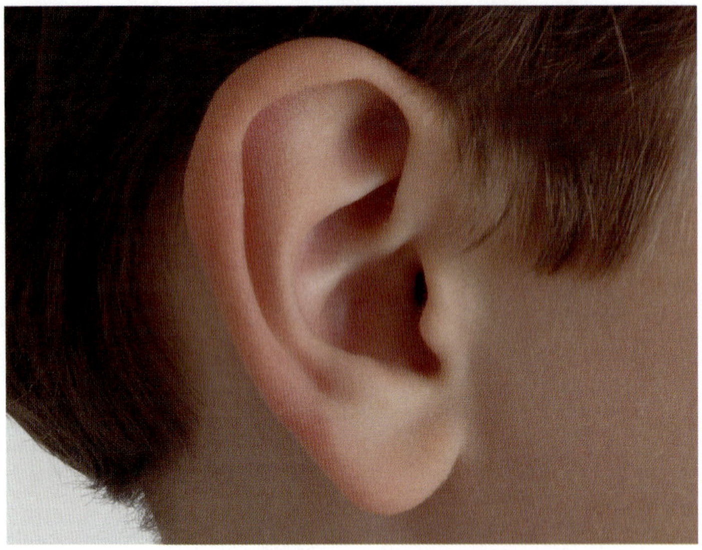

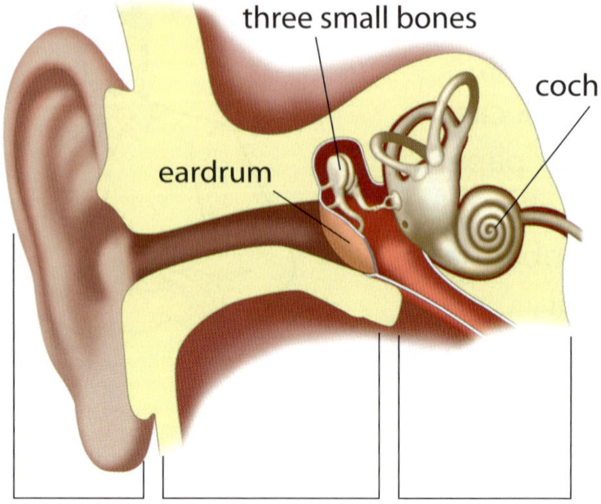

CD1 30

How do we hear? Sounds enter the outer ear and go into the middle ear. The eardrum vibrates. These vibrations travel along the three small bones to the cochlea. In the cochlea, the vibrations are turned into signals. Nerves carry these signals to our brain, and this is what we hear.

1 CD1 28 **Listen and identify the sounds.**

2 **Copy and complete the chart.**

cochlea ear three small bones eardrum

Outer ear	Middle ear	Inner ear

3 **Now use the words in the chart to copy and complete the text.**

First, sounds enter the outer ______ . Next they make the ______ vibrate. The vibrations travel along ______ . Finally, the ______ sends signals to the brain.

4 **Copy and label the picture of the ear.**

CD1 31

Our **nose** is the organ of smell. We can identify good and bad smells. Air enters the nose through two holes called the **nostrils**. This air goes to the **olfactory nerve**. The olfactory nerve detects smells in the air and sends this information to our brain. This is what we smell.

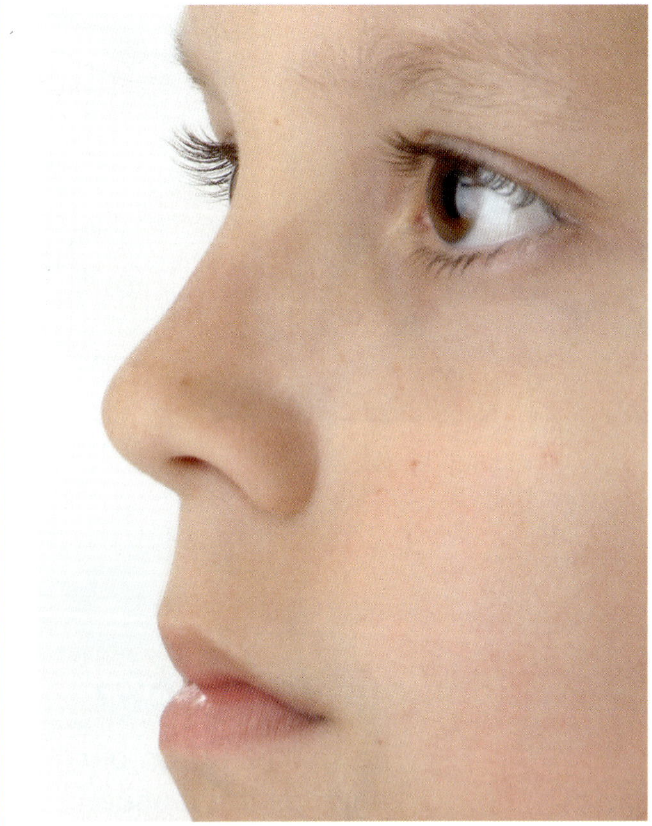

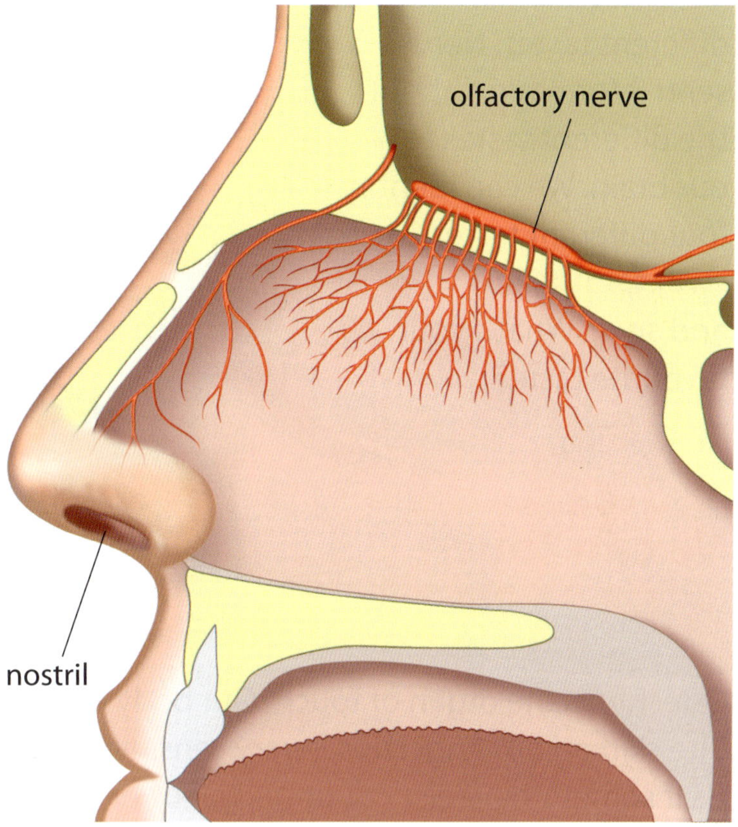

1 Me What things do you think smell good and what things smell bad?

2 How do we smell? Copy and complete the text.

smells	brain	olfactory nerve	nostrils

First, air goes into our ______ . Then, the ______ detects ______ .
This information is sent to our ______ .

3 Copy and label the picture of the nose.

DID YOU KNOW?

Our sense of smell is linked to our sense of taste. This is why we can't taste our food properly when we have a cold!

We can taste

Our **tongue** is the organ of taste. Our tongue is covered in many **taste buds**. These taste buds identify different tastes. Nerves send information about the different tastes to our brain. We can identify four different tastes: **sweet**, **salty**, **bitter** and **sour**. What's your favourite taste?

a

b

c

d

We can touch

Our **skin** is the organ of touch. Our body is covered in skin. The skin on our fingertips is very sensitive. Our skin can tell us if something feels **soft** or **hard**, **hot** or **cold**, **rough** or **smooth**. Nerves send this information to our brain.

DID YOU KNOW?

The small lines on our fingertips are unique. We can identify a person by taking their fingerprints.

1 **What do our taste buds do?**

2 **Identify the foods a–d. How do they taste?**

3 **How do you think the objects in the photos feel?**

a

b

c

d

This object feels ...

The nervous system

CD1 34

The **nervous system** controls everything we do: thinking, walking, talking, sleeping, eating, and even breathing! The most important part of the nervous system is our **brain**. The brain is an organ inside our head. It sends information to different parts of our body through the **nerves**. It also receives information from our five senses through the nerves. We have nerves all over our body.

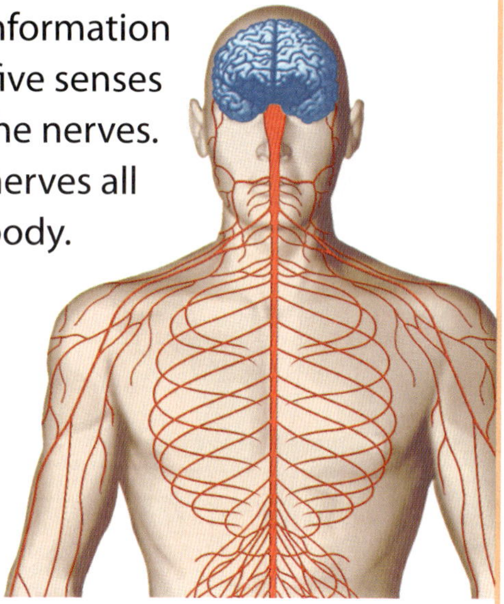

Our ears hear the alarm clock.

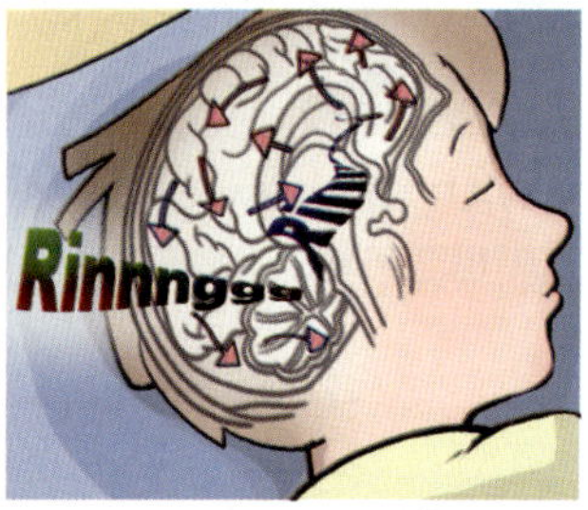

Nerves carry the information from our ears to our brain.

Our brain sends signals through our nerves to different parts of our body, and these body parts respond.

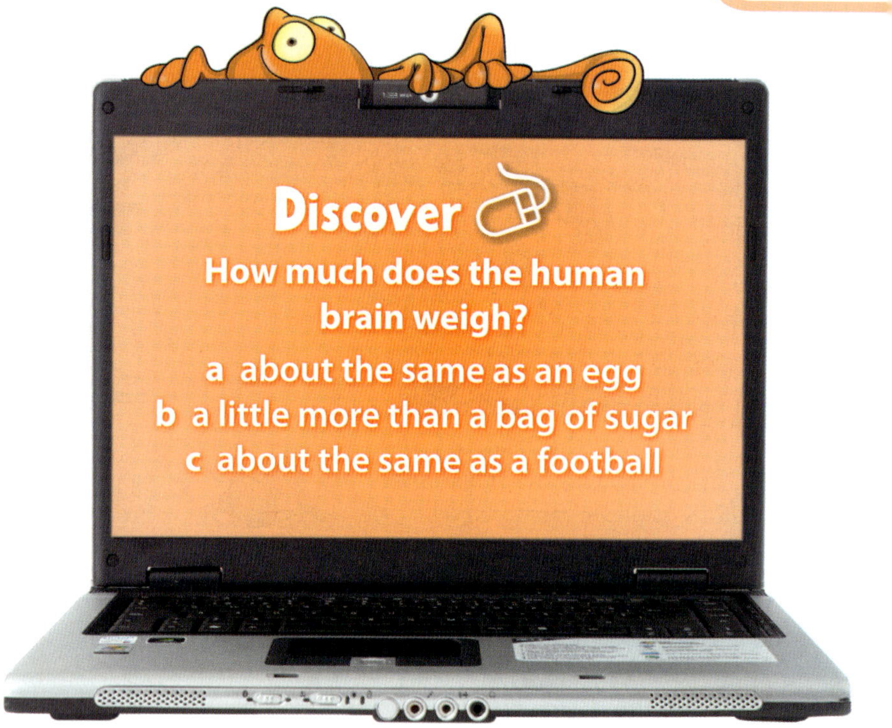

Discover

How much does the human brain weigh?

a about the same as an egg
b a little more than a bag of sugar
c about the same as a football

1 Copy and complete the sentences.

nerves   brain   nervous system

a The ______ controls our body.
b The ______ receives information from our five senses.
c The senses send information to the brain through our ______.

2 Me **How does your body respond to these things?**

a

b

c

d

A visit to the optician's

It's important to have our eyes tested regularly, especially when we're growing. If we have a problem with our sight, an eye test helps the optician find out exactly what the problem is.

During an eye test, the optician asks us to read letters, and examines our eyes. If we need glasses, the optician finds the best glasses for our eyes. Children should have an eye test at least every two years.

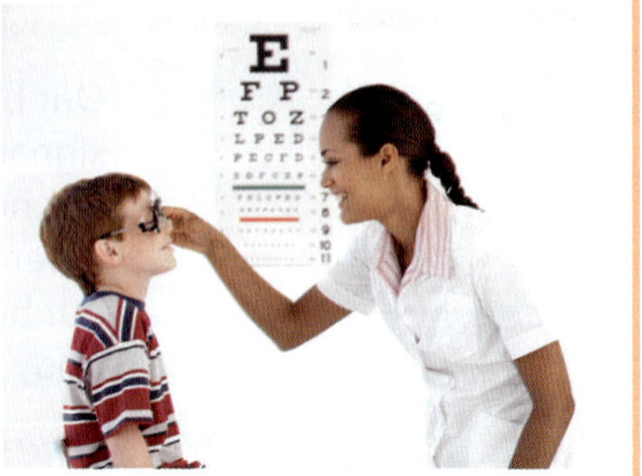

HOW I USE MY SENSES

1 Think about what you do every day.

2 Which senses do you use to do these things?

3 Write a text about how you use your senses every day.

4 Take photos or draw pictures to illustrate your text.

a

b

c

d

REMEMBER!

I use *my* tongue to taste ...

a I use my tongue to taste my food at school. I use my nose to smell my food, too!

b I use my skin to touch my pet dog.

c I use my eyes to look at my book when I do my homework.

d I use my ears to listen to my friends.

Learning to learn

1 Copy and complete the word maps.

brain eyes taste hearing skin nose

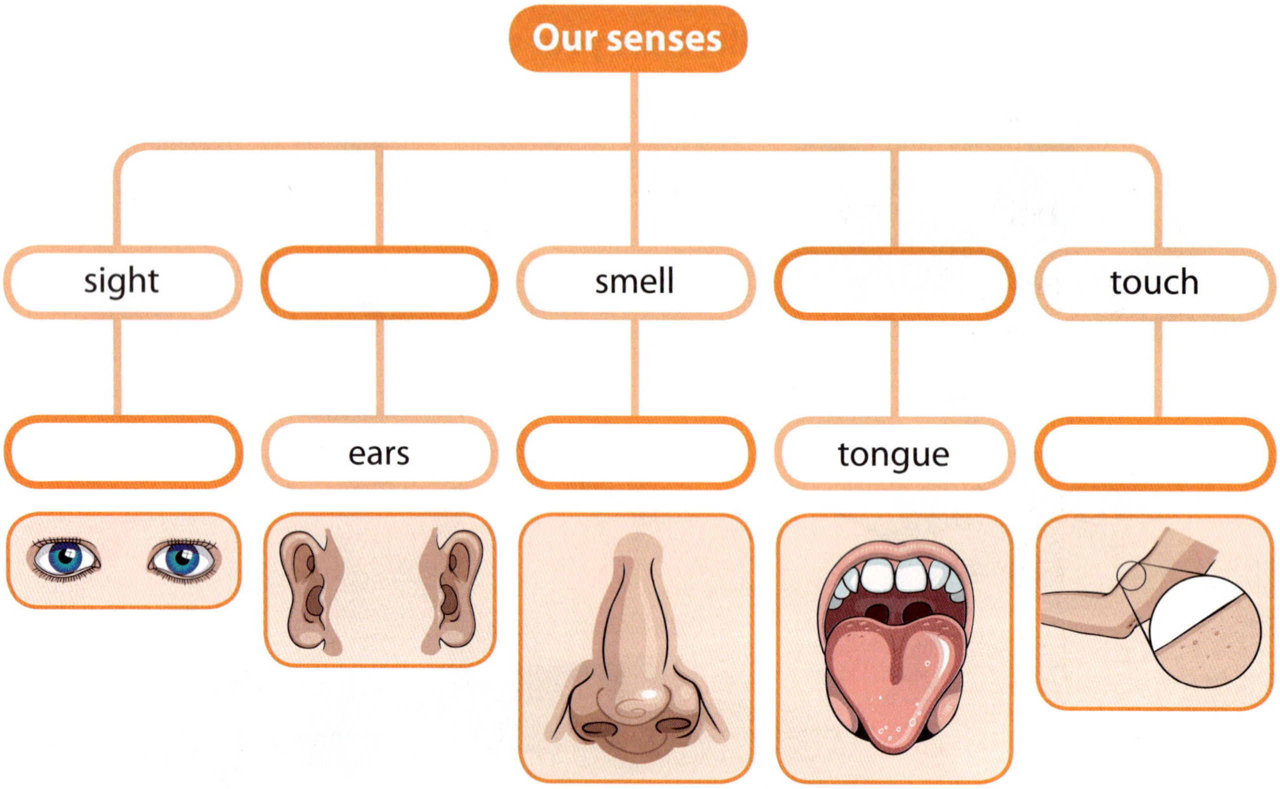

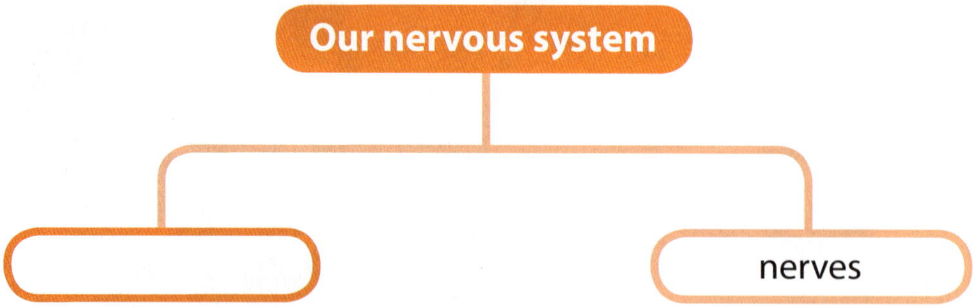

2 Copy and complete the sentences with the five sense organs.

a We can feel things with our ________ .

b Our ________ are the organs of sight.

c We use our ________ to hear.

d Our ________ can identify different tastes.

e We identify smells with our ________ .

3 Copy and complete the sentences.

brain nerves nervous system

a The ______ controls everything we do.
b The ______ is an organ inside our head.
c Our brain receives information from our senses through the ______ .

4 Copy and label the pictures of the eye.

eyebrow eyelashes eyelid | retina pupil iris

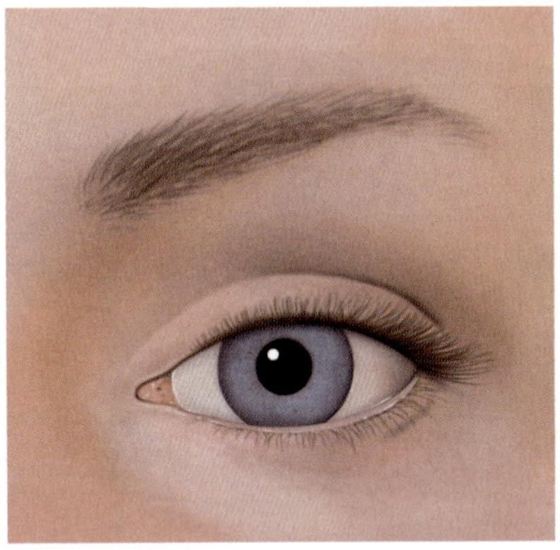

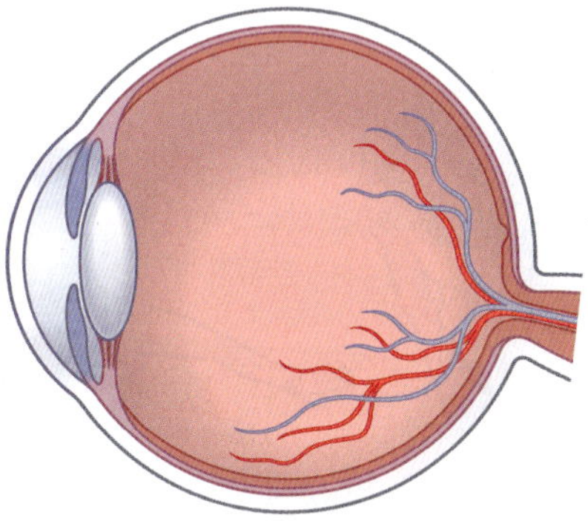

5 Copy and label the picture of the nose.

olfactory nerve nostril

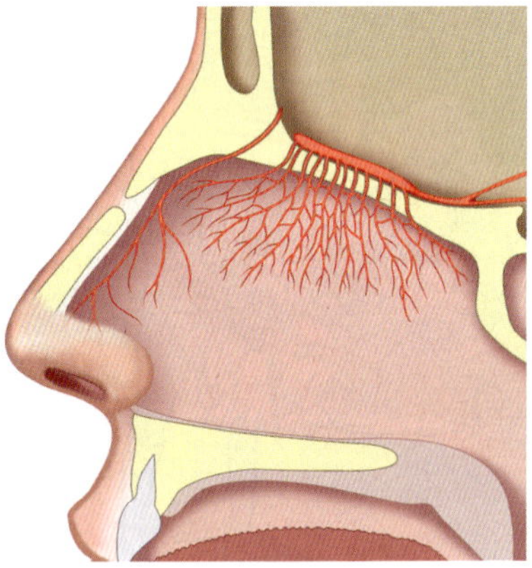

6 Order and copy the sentences about how we hear.

The cochlea sends the information to the brain.

The vibrations travel along three small bones.

The ear drum vibrates.

Sounds enter the ear.

I can name the five senses and the sense organs. ☆ ☆ ☆
I can identify the parts of the eye, ear and nose. ☆ ☆ ☆
I know how our sense organs work. ☆ ☆ ☆
I understand how the nervous system works. ☆ ☆ ☆

3 We can move

How we move our body

In this unit we're going to learn about the human body. Can you identify the joints some of the acrobats in the picture are using to move?

Our body is made up of our head, torso and limbs, and we can move our body in many ways. We can stand up and sit down, walk, run and jump. We can move our faces to smile and to eat. The **locomotor system** is what lets us move the different parts of our body and allows us to move around. The locomotor system includes **bones**, **joints** and **muscles**. All the bones in our body make up the **skeleton**. We have muscles around many of these bones, and most bones are connected at joints. Muscles and joints allow us to move our bones.

1 **Listen to Clara and Nico at the circus and identify the acrobats.**

2 **Copy and match the joints to the parts of the body.**

elbow	head	ankle
shoulder	torso	knee
neck	limbs	
wrist		hip

3 **Identify the parts of the locomotor system.**

bone joint muscle

a

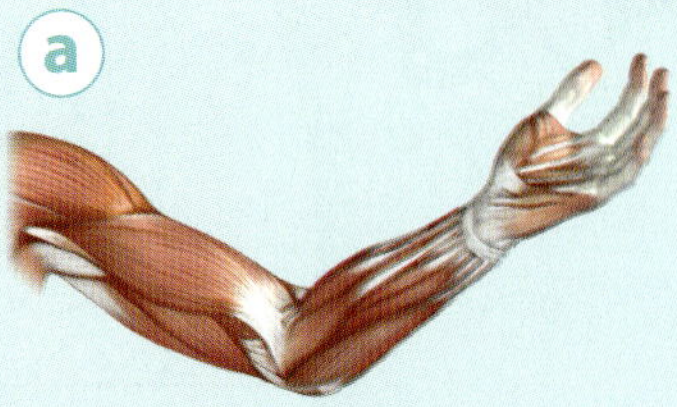

b

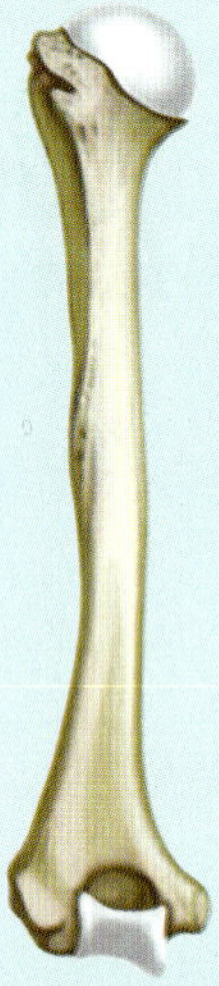

c

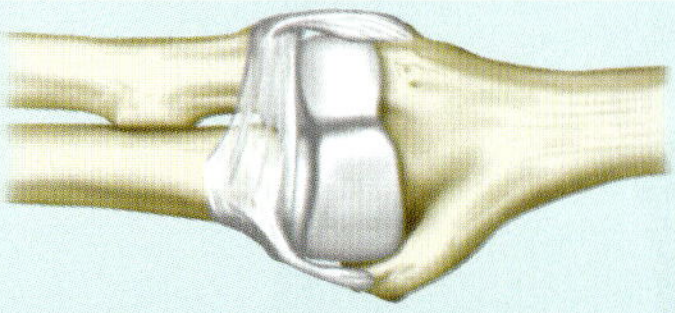

4 **Copy and complete the text.**

The locomotor system allows us to move. It includes ________, ________ and ________.

Bones: The skeleton

CD1 39

The **skeleton** is made up of all the **bones** in our body. An adult has 206 bones, but a baby has more. This is because some of our bones join together as we grow. Bones are **hard** and **rigid**. They're very strong and they don't bend.

The skeleton has three parts: the **skull**, the **torso** and the **limbs**. And the skeleton has two functions: it **supports** our body and it **protects** the delicate organs inside our body. The **skull** protects our brain and the **ribs** protect our heart and lungs.

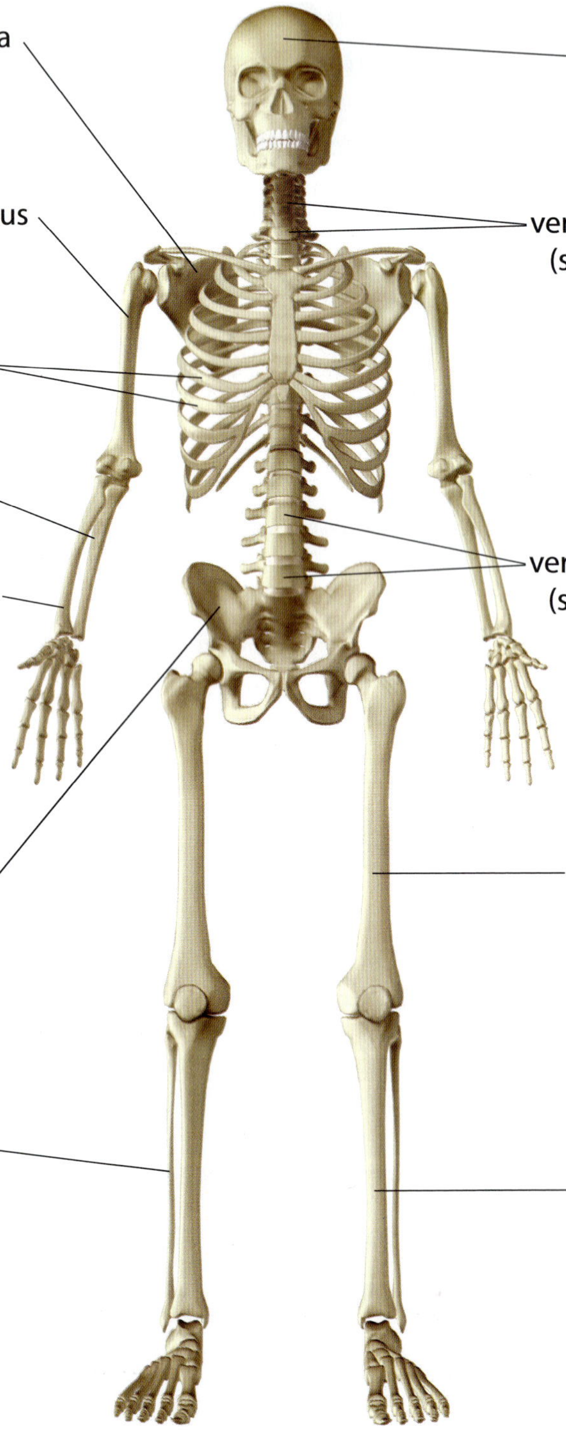

DID YOU KNOW?

A baby has about 300 bones!

1. **How many bones does an adult skeleton have?**
2. **Choose the correct words and write the sentence.**
   Bones are **soft** / **hard** and **rigid** / **flexible**.
3. **What are the two functions of the skeleton?**
   The two functions of the skeleton are . . .
4. CD1 40 **Say the *Bones* chant.**
5. CD1 41 **Sing the *Bones* song.**
6. **Copy the chart and classify the bones in the skeleton.**

Head	Torso	Limbs

Bones: Different types of bones

The **bones** in our body are all different shapes. There are three types of bones: some are **long**, some are **short** and others are **flat**. There are long bones in our arms and legs. There are short bones in our spine, hands and feet. Our skull is made up of flat bones.

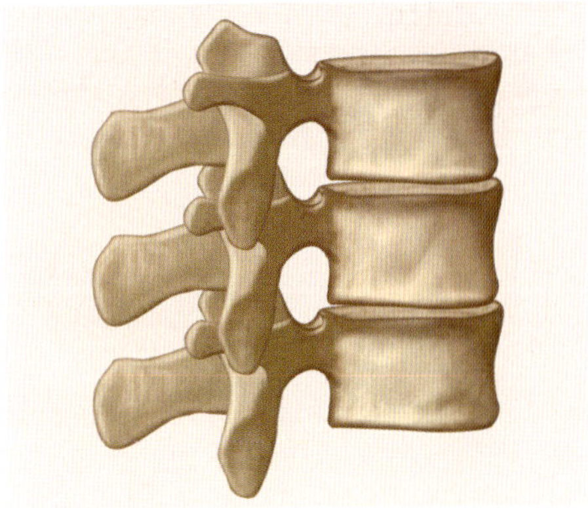

Vertebrae are short bones.

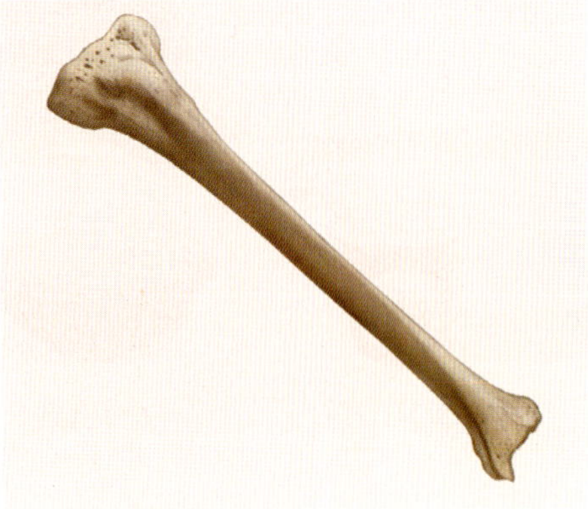

The tibia is a long bone.

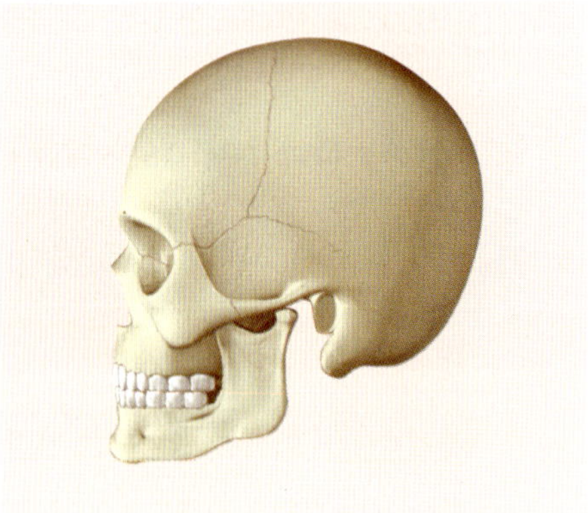

The bones in the skull are flat.

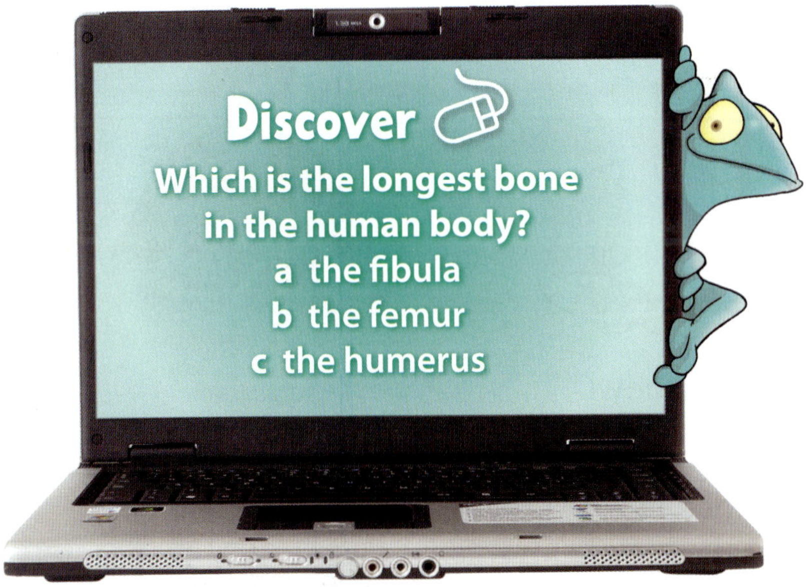

DID YOU KNOW?

The smallest bone in the human body is in our ear!

1 Copy the chart and classify the bones.

ulna vertebrae skull
femur scapula hand bones

Long bones	Short bones	Flat bones

2 Which is the odd one out? Why?

a **tibia / ribs / femur**

b **scapula / ulna / humerus**

c **pelvis / fibula / vertebrae**

. . . is the odd one out because . . .

3 Me How long is your radius?

My radius is ______ centimetres long.

What bones are made of

1 CD1 43 **Listen to the dialogue and complete the sentence.**

Milk has lots of ______, which is good for our ______.

2 Identify the foods with calcium in them.

salmon

broccoli

yoghurt

crisps

cheese

burger

Let's investigate! What are bones made of?

Investigate why we need calcium.

You need:

- a cooked chicken bone
- vinegar
- a bowl

a Observe the bone. Copy and complete Day 1 of the chart.

b Put the bone in a bowl and pour on the vinegar. Leave the bone for three days.

c Take the bone out of the vinegar. Observe it and copy and complete Day 3 of the chart.

	What colour is the bone?	What happens if you scratch the bone?	Does the bone contain lots of calcium?
Day 1			
Day 3			

d Results: Do we need calcium for strong and healthy bones?

a

b

c

CD1 44

Can you remember the names of some **joints** in our body? Our bones are connected at joints, and some joints allow our bones to move a lot. We call these **flexible joints**. The joints in our knees, elbows and shoulders are all flexible joints. Some joints only let our bones move a little. We call these **semi-flexible joints**. Our spine has semi-flexible joints. Some bones are connected at joints that can't move. We call these **fixed joints**. The joints in our skull are fixed joints.

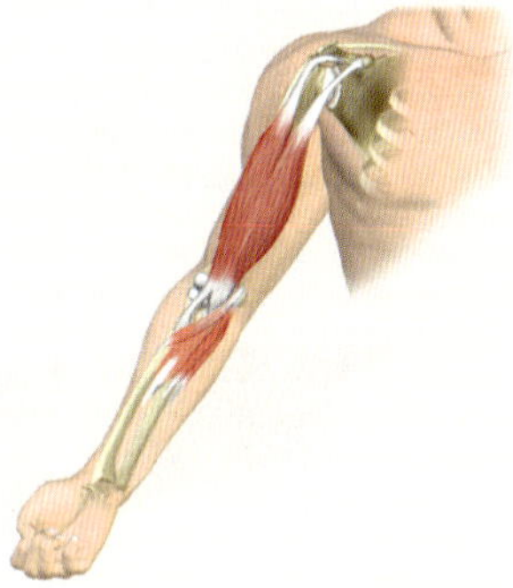
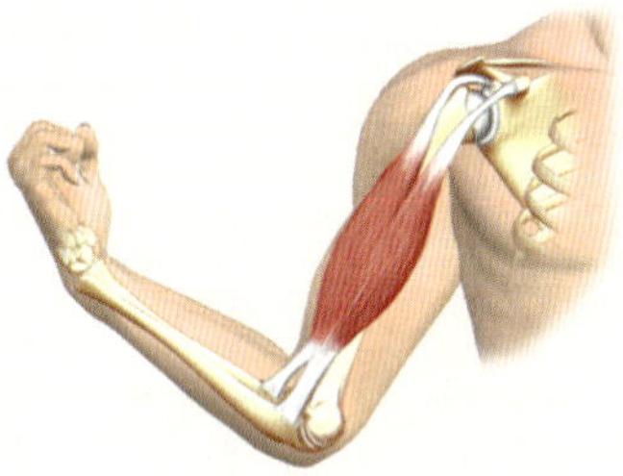

The joint in the elbow is a **flexible joint**.

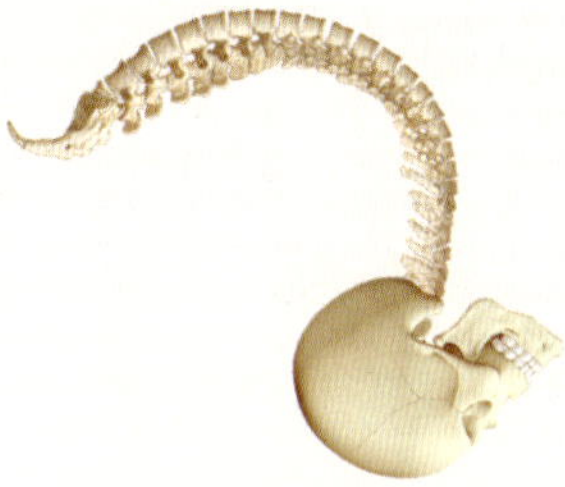

The vertebrae in the spine are **semi-flexible joints**.

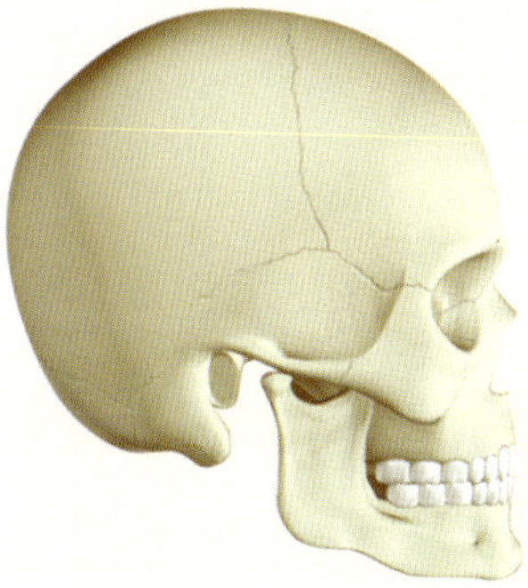

There are **fixed joints** in the skull.

1 **How can we classify joints?**

2 **Identify the joints. Are they flexible, semi-flexible or fixed?**

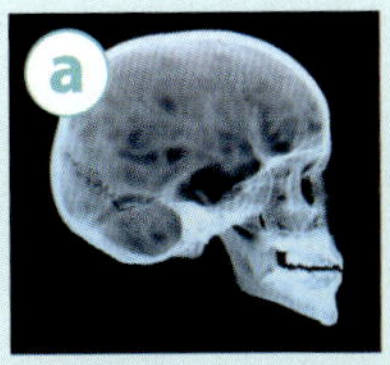

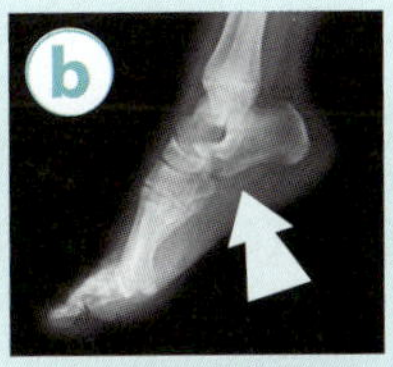

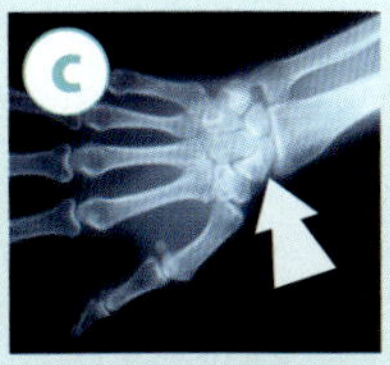

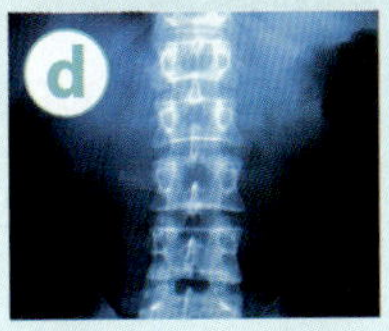

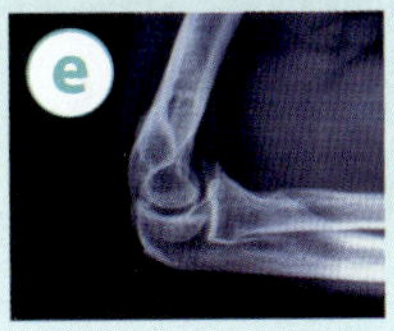

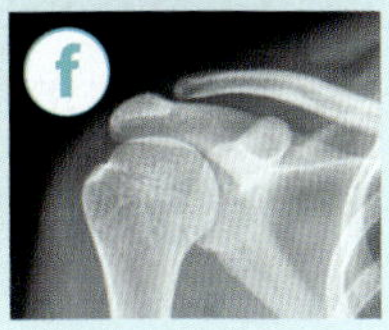

Muscles

CD1 46

Muscles are **soft** when relaxed. Most muscles are connected to bones. They move our bones by **contracting** and **relaxing**. When muscles contract, they get shorter, and when they **relax**, they get longer. The **biceps** and the **triceps** work together. When the biceps contract, the triceps relax. When the triceps contract, the biceps relax.

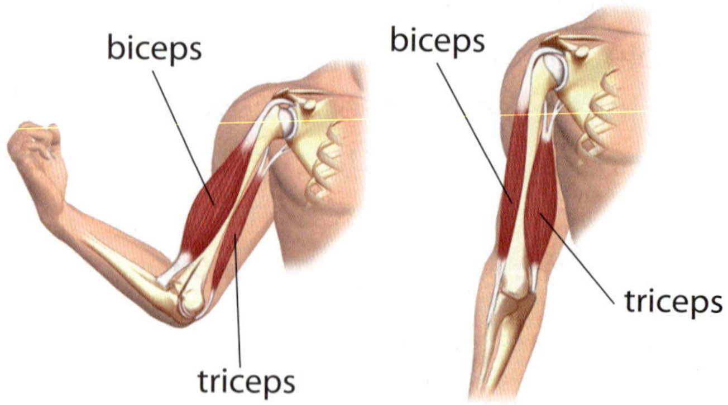

CD1 47

We have two types of muscles: **voluntary** and **involuntary**. We can move voluntary muscles when we want. We decide to do something and our brain sends a signal to these muscles.

We can't control involuntary muscles. They move automatically. Our **heart** is an involuntary muscle. It moves all the time without us thinking about it. There are also involuntary muscles in our stomach that help us digest our food.

We use our muscles to dance.

Our heart is moving all the time, even when we're asleep!

1 Copy and complete the sentence.

Muscles move our bones by ______ and ______.

2 Copy and complete the sentences using *contract* and *relax*.

a When I bend my arm, my biceps ______ and my triceps ______.

b When I stretch my arm, my triceps ______ and my biceps ______.

3 Match and write the sentences.

a Voluntary muscles	move automatically.
b Involuntary muscles	move when we want.

The muscles in our body

CD1 49

There are over six hundred **muscles** in our body, and every muscle has a special function.

In our arms there are **biceps** and **triceps**. We use these muscles to write, play tennis and pick things up.

In our legs there are **biceps**, **quadriceps** and **calf muscles**. These muscles help us walk, run and jump.

In our shoulders there are **deltoids**. The **trapezius** muscle is in our back. It helps us move our arms.

In our chest there are **pectorals**. Our **abdominals** are near our stomach. These muscles help us bend down.

We also have many muscles in our face. The **masseter** helps us chew our food.

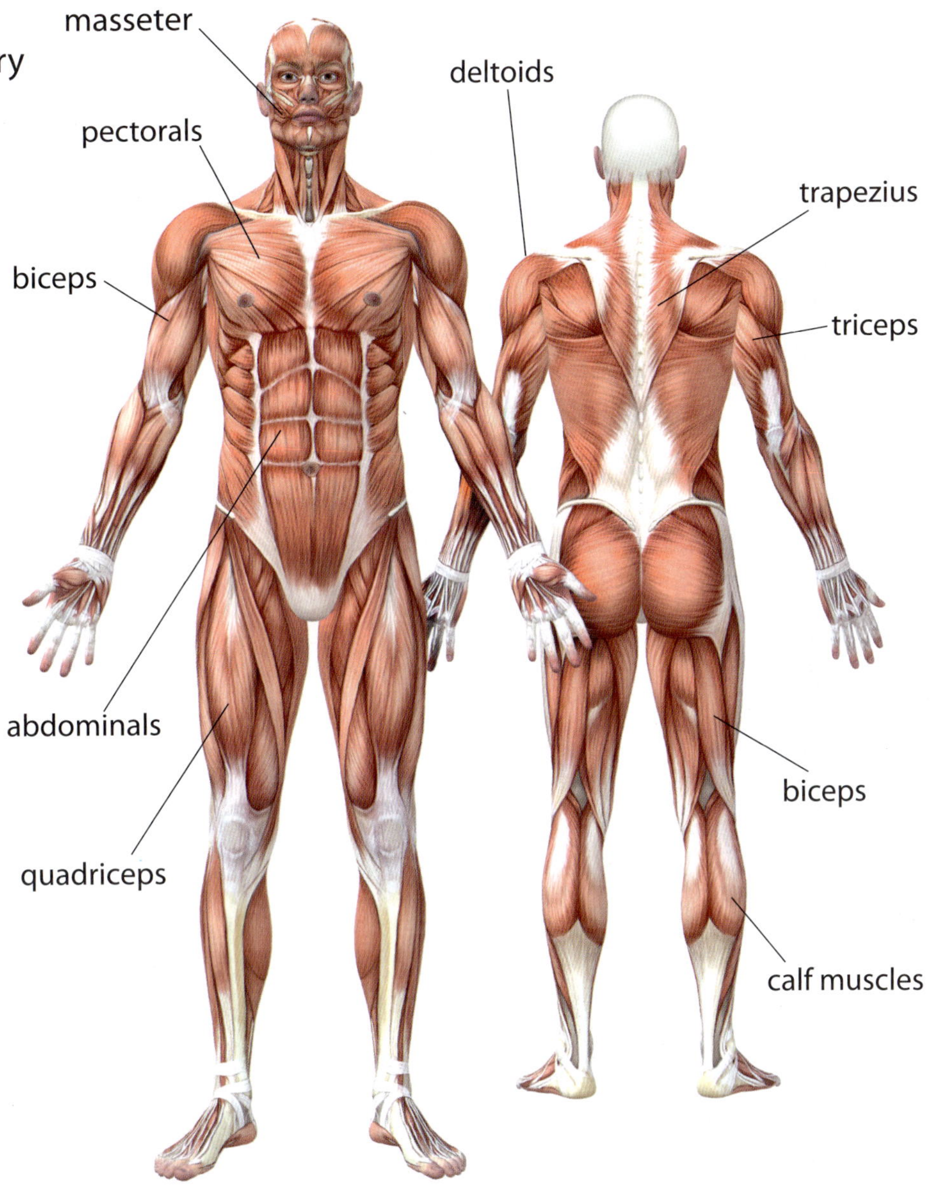

chew *(verb)* to use your teeth to bite food into small pieces so you can swallow it.

1 CD1 48 **Say the *Muscles* chant.**

2 **Copy the chart and classify the muscles.**

Arms	Legs	Torso	Head

The P.E. class

CD1 50

CD1 51

A pulled muscle can happen if we stretch a muscle too much. It's important to warm up our muscles before we exercise. Warm-up exercises help stretch our muscles. If we pull a muscle, it's important to rest it.

MY SCIENCE PROJECT

WHAT MY BODY NEEDS

1 **Your body needs food, exercise and rest.**

2 **Keep a diary for one week about the things that you do every day to look after your body.**

- a Do you have a balanced diet and eat regular meals?
- b Do you do regular exercise?
- c Do you have enough rest?

3 **After one week, write about how you look after your body.**

On Monday I go to my swimming class after school.

On Tuesday I walk to school. I eat a healthy lunch. I have chicken and vegetables!

On Wednesday I have fruit for breakfast. I have an apple and a banana, and I have cereals.

On Thursday ...

Learning to learn

1 Copy and complete the word map.

involuntary semi-flexible soft hard muscles

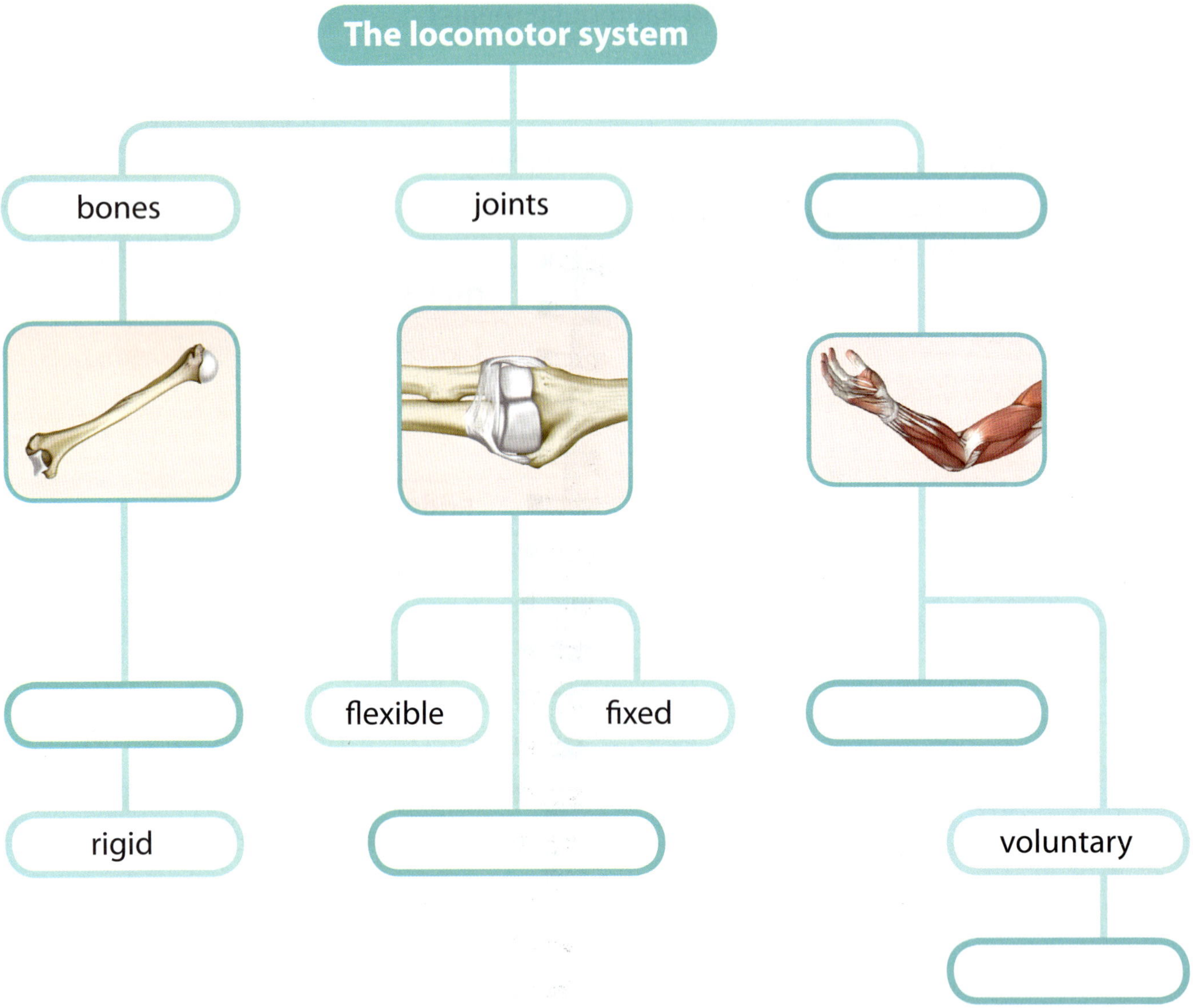

2 Use the word map to copy and complete the sentences.

a Our locomotor system contains bones, ______ and ______ .

b Our bones are hard and ______ .

c There are ______ , semi-flexible and fixed joints.

d Our muscles are ______ when relaxed.

e There are ______ and involuntary muscles.

3 Match and write the sentences.

a The locomotor system — allows us to move our body and move around.
b The skeleton
c Muscles
d Joints
e Bones

can be flexible, semi-flexible or fixed.
allows us to move our body and move around.
are hard and rigid.
are soft when relaxed.
is made up of all the bones in our body.

4 Which is the odd one out? Why?

a masseter / fibula / abdominals
b biceps / skull / femur
c triceps / radius / deltoids
d pectorals / trapezius / ulna

... is the odd one out because ...

5 Copy and complete the chart.

vertebrae radius skull

Long bones	Short bones	Flat bones

6 Copy the pictures and label the muscles that are contracting and relaxing.

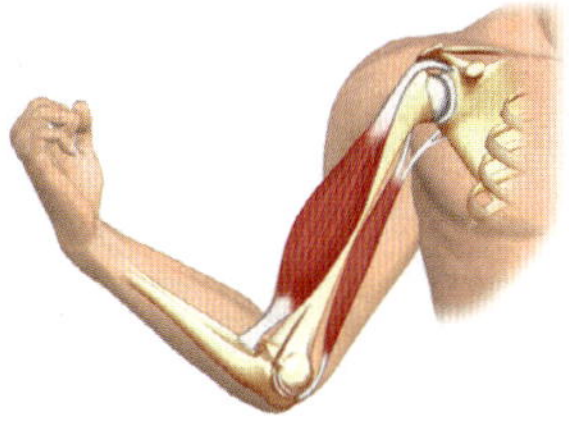

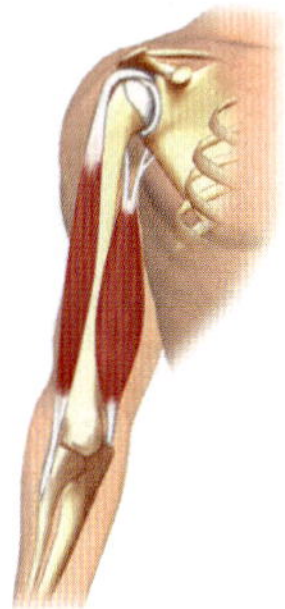

I know about the locomotor system. ☆ ☆ ☆

I know the names and characteristics of some bones. ☆ ☆ ☆

I can name three types of joints. ☆ ☆ ☆

I know the names and characteristics of some muscles. ☆ ☆ ☆

I know the functions of some muscles. ☆ ☆ ☆

4 Animals

Classifying animals

In this unit we're going to learn more about classifying animals.

This animal has four legs and fur. It's a carnivore and it can run. Look at the photos. Which animal is it?

CD1 53

We can classify animals in different ways. One way is to classify animals into **vertebrates** and **invertebrates**. Vertebrates have a backbone, and invertebrates don't have a backbone.

We can also classify vertebrates into five smaller groups: **mammals**, **birds**, **fish**, **reptiles** and **amphibians**.

CD1 55

There are many different types of invertebrates. Some invertebrates have a **shell**, some have an **exoskeleton** and others have a **soft body**.

1 (CD1 52) **Say the *Vertebrates* chant.**

2 Copy and complete the sentences.

Invertebrates Vertebrates

a ______ have a backbone.

b ______ don't have a backbone.

3 (CD1 54) **Say the *Animals* chant.**

4 Match and write the sentences.

a chameleon	mammal
b toad	bird
c monkey	fish
d shark	reptile
e eagle	amphibian

A chameleon is a reptile.

Vertebrates

CD1 56

Dogs, dolphins and bats are **mammals**. Their babies are born live, and all baby mammals drink their mother's milk. Most mammals have four legs. All mammals breathe with their lungs.

All **birds** have feathers, a beak and wings. Most birds can fly, but some can swim or run. All birds lay eggs and breathe with their lungs.

Most **reptiles** live on land. Some have bodies covered in scales, but others have a shell. Some reptiles have legs and some reptiles have no legs. Reptiles lay eggs and breathe with their lungs.

Fish live in water. They have fins, scales and gills. They breathe through their gills. Most fish lay eggs.

Amphibians lay eggs. Their babies live in water and breathe through their gills. Adult amphibians live on land and in water. They breathe through their lungs and moist skin. Adult amphibians have four legs.

1 Copy and complete the sentences.

a Mammals, birds, reptiles and adult amphibians breathe with their _____.

b Fish and baby amphibians breathe through their _____.

2 Match and write the sentences.

a	Mammals	have feathers, a beak and wings.
b	Birds	can live on land and in water.
c	Fish	have scales, and some have a shell.
d	Reptiles	are born live and drink their mother's milk.
e	Amphibians	have scales and breathe through their gills.

3 Write a text about a vertebrate animal.

CD1 57

Invertebrates are the biggest group of animals on Earth. They can be classified into many smaller groups, but they all have one common characteristic: invertebrates **don't have a backbone**.

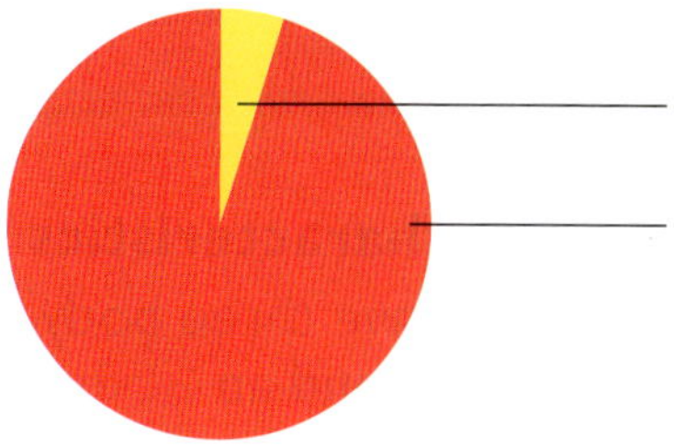

CD1 58

Some invertebrates, like worms, have a **soft body** and often hide under rocks for protection. Other invertebrates, like snails and mussels, have a **shell** to protect their body.

Many invertebrates have an **exoskeleton**. This is like a skeleton outside the body, which supports and protects the invertebrate. Insects, spiders and millipedes have a **thin exoskeleton**, and crabs and lobsters have a **thick exoskeleton**.

Invertebrates are different in other ways, too. Spiders have eight legs, insects have six legs and millipedes have hundreds of legs!

Like many vertebrates, invertebrates **lay eggs**.

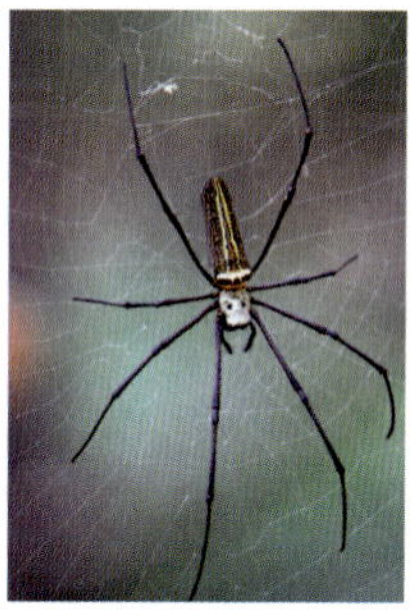

1 **Are there more vertebrates or invertebrates on Earth?**

2 **Copy and complete the sentence.**

shell	body	exoskeleton

Invertebrates can have a soft ______, a ______ or an ______.

3 CD1 59 **Say the *Invertebrates* rap.**

4 **Write a text about an invertebrate animal.**

DID YOU KNOW?

The *Illacme plenipes* millipede can have 700 legs!

Let's investigate! Insects

CD1 60

http://

SCIENCE CLUB

Animals

Invertebrates

Insects

Physical characteristics

Symmetry

Diet

Reproduction

Physical characteristics

- Insects have three body parts: a **head**, a **thorax** and an **abdomen**.
- Insects have **antennae** on their heads. They use their antennae to touch, smell or taste.
- Insects have **six legs** that are connected to the thorax.
- Some insects have one or two pairs of **wings**. Others don't have wings. The wings are also connected to the thorax.

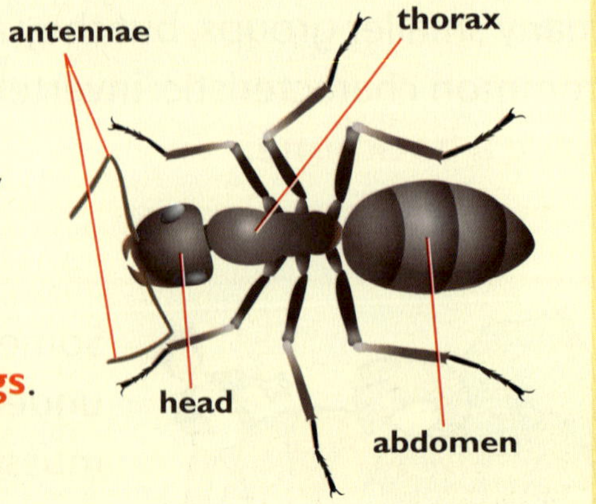

Symmetry

- An insect's body is symmetrical. This means that it's the same on each side.

Diet

- Some insects, like dragonflies, are carnivores.
- Some insects, like grasshoppers, are herbivores.

Reproduction

- Insects lay eggs. Baby insects are called **larvae**.
- Some larvae transform into adult insects by getting bigger and bigger, sometimes growing wings.

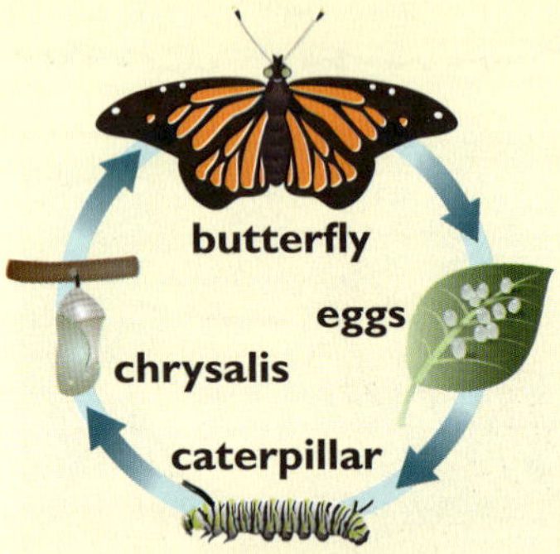

- Some larvae transform into adult insects inside a **pupa**. This is called a **chrysalis** in butterflies.
- The transformation into an adult insect is called **metamorphosis**.

Investigate insects. Use the internet to investigate and write about an insect.

a Find information about its physical characteristics.

b Where does it live?

c What does it eat?

d How does it reproduce?

e Find photos or draw pictures to illustrate your text.

How animals reproduce

Animals reproduce in two ways. Mammals are **viviparous**, which means they have live babies.

Other animals lay eggs. We call these animals **oviparous**. Invertebrates, birds, fish, reptiles and amphibians are oviparous.

incubate *(verb)* to keep eggs warm while the baby grows inside.

DID YOU KNOW?

Some animals incubate their eggs to keep them warm.

1 **Identify the viviparous and oviparous animals in photos a–g.**

2 **Copy and complete the chart.**

Viviparous animals	Oviparous animals

3 **What are these animals doing?**

What do animals eat?

CD1 62

We can classify animals by what they eat. **Herbivores** eat plants, **carnivores** eat other animals, and **omnivores** eat plants and other animals.

Herbivores eat different parts of plants, such as leaves, roots, stems, fruit and seeds. Rabbits and giraffes are herbivores.

Tigers and crocodiles are **carnivores**. They eat other animals.

Hens and bears are **omnivores**. Hens eat seeds and invertebrates. Bears eat fruit, insects and fish.

What do you eat? Are you a herbivore, a carnivore or an omnivore?

1 Identify the herbivores, carnivores and omnivores in the pictures.

2 Copy and complete the sentences.

Omnivores Carnivores Herbivores

a ______ eat plants.
b ______ eat other animals.
c ______ eat plants and other animals.

3 Copy and complete the chart. Write sentences.

Herbivores	Carnivores	Omnivores

A giraffe is a …

Animal coverings

CD1 64

Animals have different coverings. These coverings are for protection. All animals have **skin**. Skin is waterproof and protects muscles, bones and organs.

Fur is made up of hair. Some mammals, like polar bears, have a lot of hair, and other mammals, like whales, have very little hair. Fur traps warm air against the skin and keeps the animal warm.

Birds need **feathers** for flying, keeping warm and attracting other birds. All feathers are waterproof.

Fish and reptiles have **scales**. Scales are waterproof, too.

CD1 65

Some animals, like chameleons, use **camouflage** to help them hide from predators. Other animals, like ladybirds, have bright colours. These bright colours tell predators that they aren't good to eat.

predator *(noun)* an animal that hunts and eats other animals.

1 CD1 63 **Say the *Animal coverings* chant.**

2 **Look at photos a–f and describe the animal coverings.**

3 **How do these coverings protect the animals?**

4 Me **What protective covering do you have? Why?**

a

b

c

d

e

f

Animals in danger

CD1 67

CD1 68

In Spain there are many protected areas, such as national parks or nature reserves. These are often places where many plants and animals live. Many protected areas are homes to protected species like the Pyrenees mountain goat, the Iberian lynx or the brown bear. These animals can live and reproduce in these areas because their surroundings are protected and people can't hunt them. Are there protected areas where you live?

Iberian lynx

My Science Presentation

ANIMALS IN DANGER

1. **Choose an animal that is in danger of extinction.**
2. **Find out about your animal using the internet and other reference sources.**
3. **Try to include the following information:**
   - a A description of your animal.
   - b Is it a vertebrate or an invertebrate?
   - c Is it a herbivore, a carnivore or an omnivore?
   - d What exactly does it eat?
   - e How does it reproduce?
   - f Where does it live?
   - g What protective covering does it have?
4. **Write a text using your information.**
5. **Find photos or draw pictures of your animal.**
6. **Use your text and your pictures to make a poster.**
7. **Present your poster to the class.**

Learning to learn

1 Copy and complete the word map.

carnivores reptiles birds invertebrates viviparous

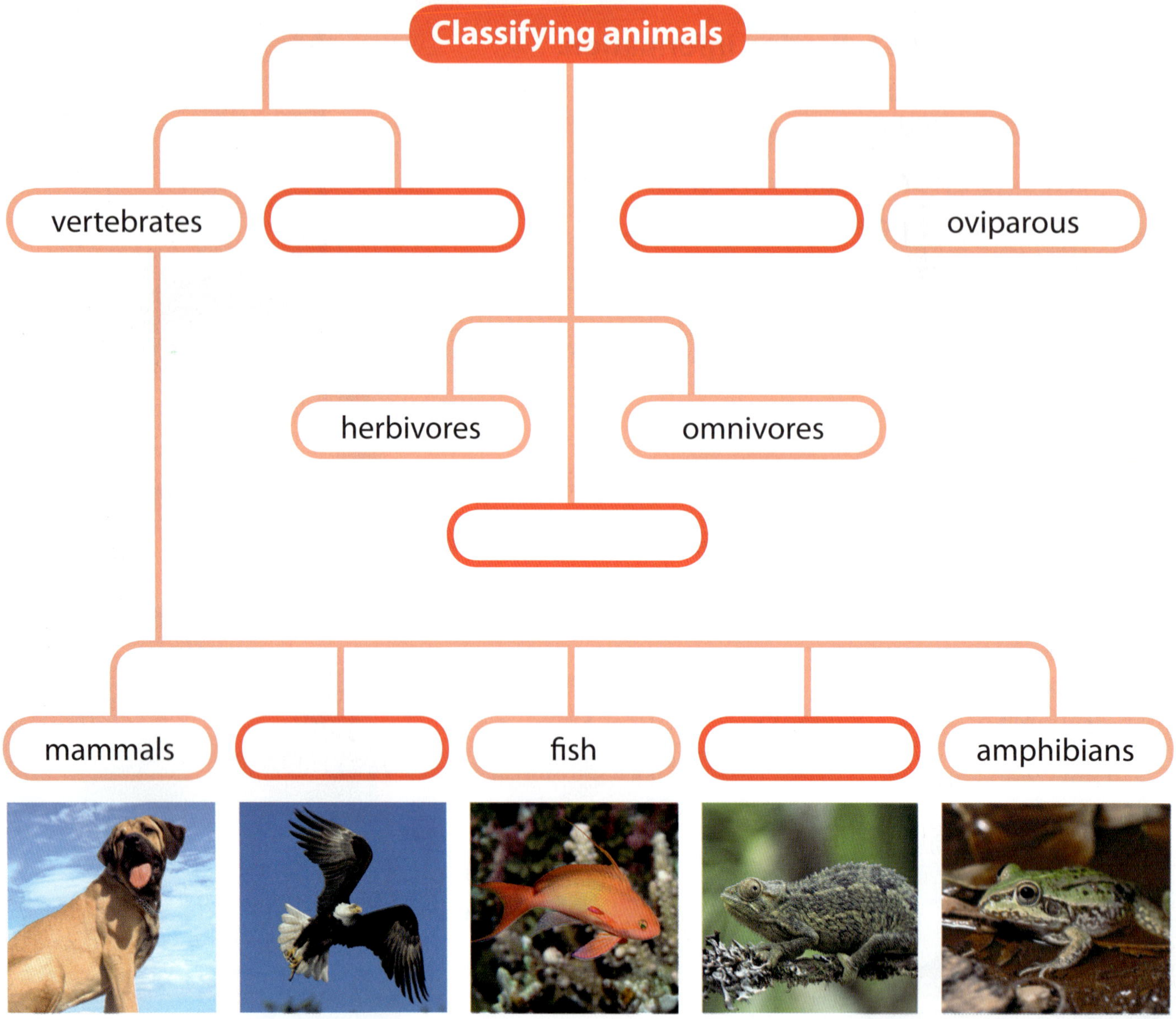

2 Use the word map to copy and complete the sentences.

a ______ have a backbone, but ______ don't.

b Vertebrates can be classified as ______, ______, ______, ______ and ______.

c Herbivores eat plants, ______ eat other animals and ______ eat plants and other animals.

d Viviparous animals are born live, but ______ animals lay eggs.

3 **Copy and complete the chart with these invertebrates.**

Shell	Exoskeleton	Soft body

4 **Which is the odd one out? Why?**

a **bear** / **rabbit** / **cow**

b **tiger** / **spider** / **giraffe**

c **monkey** / **snake** / **crocodile**

5 **Copy and complete the sentences.**

fur camouflage scales
bright colours feathers

a Crocodiles have ______ .

b Ladybirds have ______ .

c Eagles have ______ .

d Tigers have ______ .

e Chameleons use ______ .

6 **Copy the insect and label its body parts.**

head abdomen
thorax antennae

I can classify animals into vertebrates and invertebrates.	☆ ☆ ☆
I can identify herbivores, carnivores and omnivores.	☆ ☆ ☆
I know how animals reproduce.	☆ ☆ ☆
I can identify viviparous and oviparous animals.	☆ ☆ ☆
I know why animals have different coverings.	☆ ☆ ☆

Listen to the quiz and write the answers to the questions.

CD1 69

SCIENCE CLUB QUIZ

1 What are the characteristics of living things?

2 What are the three life processes of living things?

3 What are the five sense organs?

4 What carries information from our senses to our brain?

5 What are the two functions of the skeleton?

6 What are the three types of bones?

7 What are the three types of joints?

8 What are the two types of muscles?

9 What is the common characteristic of invertebrates?

10 What do we call animals that have live babies and animals that lay eggs?

Now look at units 1, 2, 3 and 4 and check your answers.

CD1 70 Listen and check your answers.

How did you do?

8–10 points	5–7 points	0–4 points
Excellent	Good	Try again

Read and answer the definitions.

SCIENCE CHALLENGE

Find a friend. Decide who is Pupil A and who is Pupil B. Take it in turns to ask and answer the questions in the Science Challenge.

PUPIL A

1. Speaking is an example of this life process.
2. Having babies is an example of this life process.
3. These are the organs of hearing.
4. This is the organ of taste.
5. This is a big coloured circle at the front of the eye.
6. We need this for strong and healthy bones.
7. These animals are vertebrates and drink their mother's milk.
8. These animals have three body parts and six legs.
9. These animals have fins and scales and breathe through their gills.
10. These animals eat plants and other animals.

PUPIL B

1. Eating is an example of this life process.
2. These are the organs of sight.
3. This is the organ of smell.
4. This is the organ of touch.
5. These joints don't move.
6. When these muscles contract, the triceps relax.
7. These animals can live on land and in water.
8. These animals have scales or a shell, breathe with their lungs and lay eggs.
9. These animals eat other animals.
10. Some animals have this to hide from predators.

Can you remember the definitions of these words?

shelter *(noun)* ...
sweat *(noun)* ...
chew *(verb)* ...
incubate *(verb)* ...
predator *(noun)* ...

Answers on Photocopiable Resources CD, Unit 4.

5 Plants — Classifying plants

CD2 2

There are many different types of plants which we can classify in different ways. One way we can classify plants is by their **stems**.

- **Grasses** have a soft stem. They are thin and flexible and are usually short.
- **Bushes** have a thick, hard stem with low branches. They are taller than grasses and live longer.
- **Trees** have a thick, hard stem called a trunk. They are the tallest plants and have high branches. Some trees can live for hundreds of years.

DID YOU KNOW?

All tree trunks have rings inside. They have one dark ring for each year of the tree's life. How old is this tree?

c

d

g

h

1 CD2 3 Say the *Plants* chant.

2 **How can you classify the plants in photos a–h?**

3 **What parts of these plants can you identify?**

4 CD2 4 Say the *Plants* rap.

5 **True or false? Copy the sentences and correct the ones that are false.**

a Grasses are thin and rigid.

b Bushes have low branches.

c Trees have thin and flexible stems.

Parts of plants

All plants have **leaves**, **stems** and **roots**.

Leaves grow from the stems or branches. Leaves use sunlight to help make their own food.

Deciduous trees lose all their leaves in autumn. Evergreen trees produce new leaves all year.

Stems carry water and minerals from the roots to the rest of the plant. They also support the plant.

Roots are the part of the plant that is underground. Roots have two functions:

- They absorb water and minerals that the plant needs to grow.
- They fix the plant into the ground.

1 What parts do plants have?

2 What are the functions of roots/stems/leaves?

3 What is the difference between deciduous trees and evergreen trees?

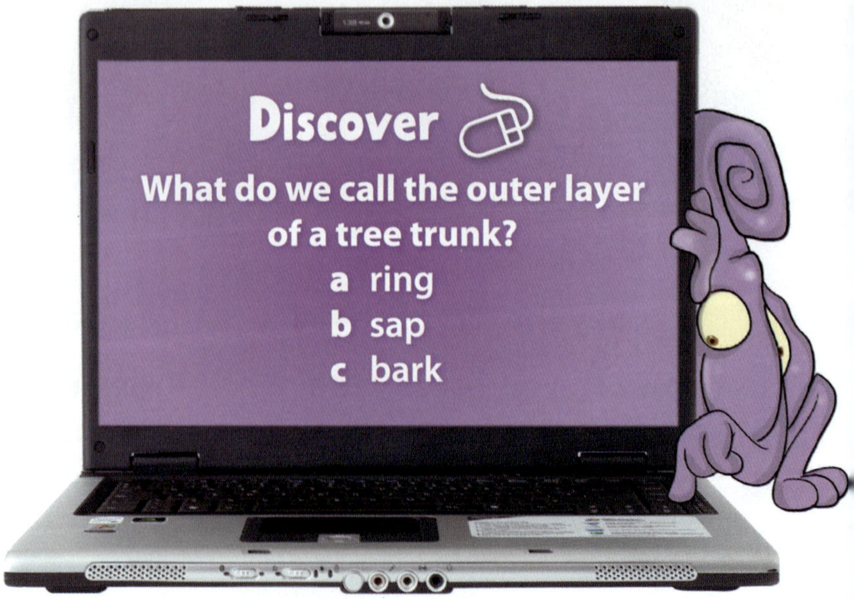

CD2 7

Fir trees are evergreens. Their trunks are tall and straight. They have fir cones. Squirrels and other animals eat the seeds from the **fir cones**.

The **blackberry bush** has lots of long branches. These branches have thorns. In the spring the blackberry bush has small pale pink flowers. In the summer it gives us **blackberries**.

Wheat is a deciduous grass. It has a long stem and many **kernels** at the end of each stem. We make bread from wheat.

thorn *(noun)* thin, sharp part of a plant.

a

b

c

1  **Why do some plants have thorns?**

2 **Identify the plants in photos a–c.**

3 **Copy and complete the chart with the information.**

4 **Add more plants to your chart.**

	What type of plant is it?	Does it have flowers?	Does it have fruit?
Fir			
Blackberry			
Wheat			

Identifying leaves

Leaves have two parts. They have a **stalk** and a **blade**. Some leaves are big and some are small.

Leaves are different shapes. This is because they have different **margins**. There are many types of margins including **entire**, **dentate**, **serrate**, **sinuate**, **lobed** and **palmate**.

entire

dentate

serrate

sinuate

lobed

palmate

Let's investigate! Identifying leaves

Investigate leaves in your environment.

Copy and complete the chart.

Leaf	Size	Margin

CD2 9

Some trees, bushes and grasses have **flowers**.

The reproductive organs of a plant are inside the flower. These organs make seeds that grow into new plants. Flowers can be different shapes, sizes and colours, but they all have common parts.

Sepals are small green leaves that protect the flower before it opens.

Petals can be many different colours. They attract insects to the flower.

The **stamens** have pollen at their ends. Insects take pollen to other flowers.

The **carpel** is the part of the flower where the seeds develop. It grows into a fruit, which has seeds inside. When the fruit falls to the ground, a new plant can grow from the seed.

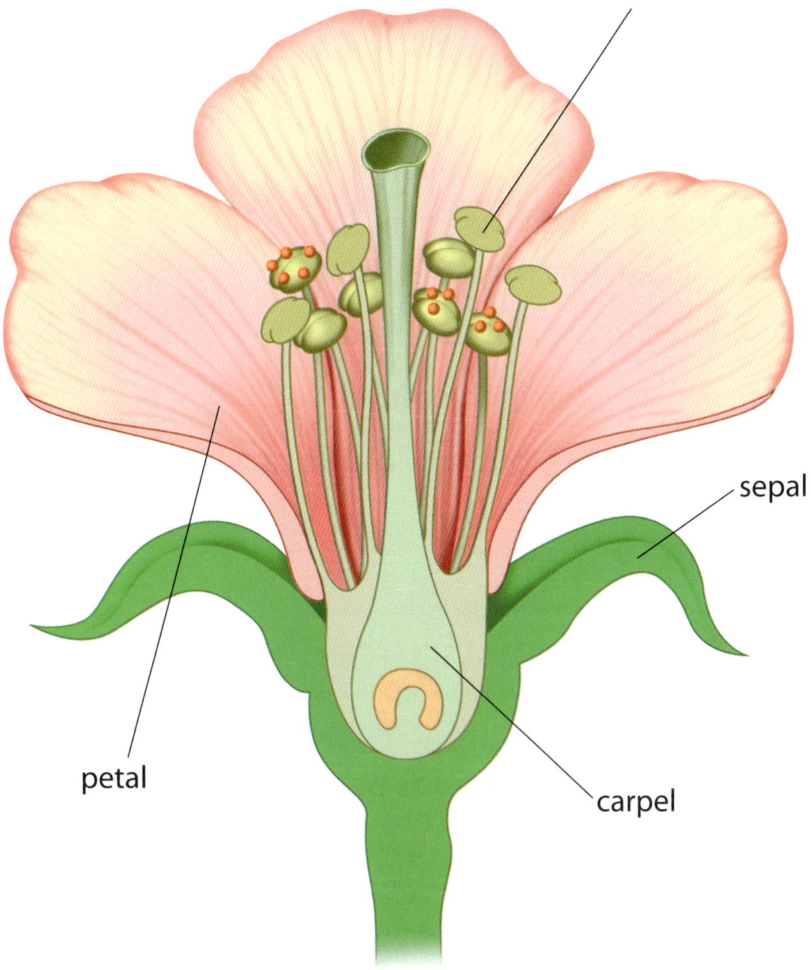

pollen *(noun)* a powder which flowers produce.

1. CD2 10 **Say the *Flower* chant.**
2. **Why do some plants have colourful petals?**
3. CD2 11 **Say the *Flower* rap.**
4. **What parts of the flowers can you identify in photos a, b and c?**

a

b

c

The life cycle of a plant

germinate *(verb)* when a shoot starts to grow from a seed.

CD2 12

1 Most seeds need warmth, water, sunlight and air to germinate.

2 Roots grow down from the seed.

3 A stem grows up.

4 Leaves grow on the stem. The plant can now make its own food.

5 A flower grows on the plant.

6 Seeds develop in the carpel.

7 The plant dies, but new plants can grow from its seeds.

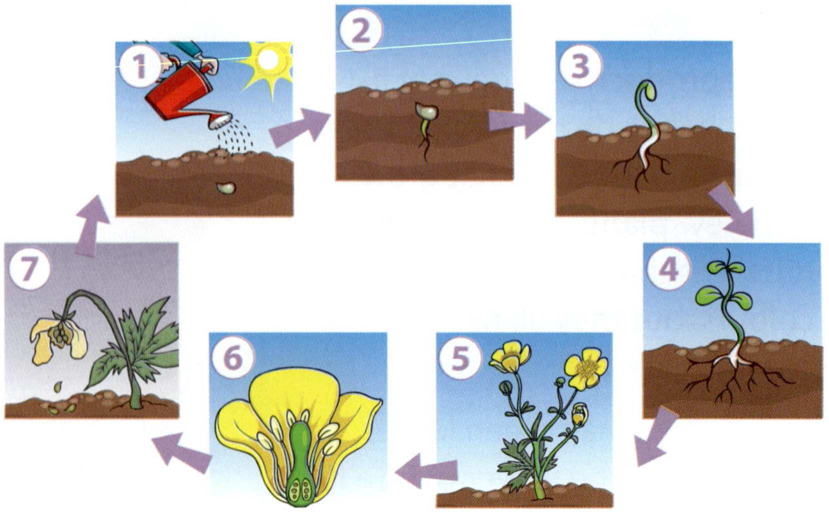

Let's investigate! What seeds need to germinate

Investigate what seeds need to germinate.

Do seeds need soil to germinate?

You need:

- 4 cups
- 3 materials (soil, cotton wool, paper)
- seeds

a Put some of each material in cups 1–3. Leave cup 4 with nothing.

b Put two seeds in each cup and water them every day.

c Do you think the seeds will germinate? Check the results after a week.

	 Soil	 Cotton wool	 Paper	 Nothing
Will it germinate?				
Results				
Conclusion	Seeds **do** / **don't** need soil to germinate.			

We need plants

a

b

c

d

e

f

g

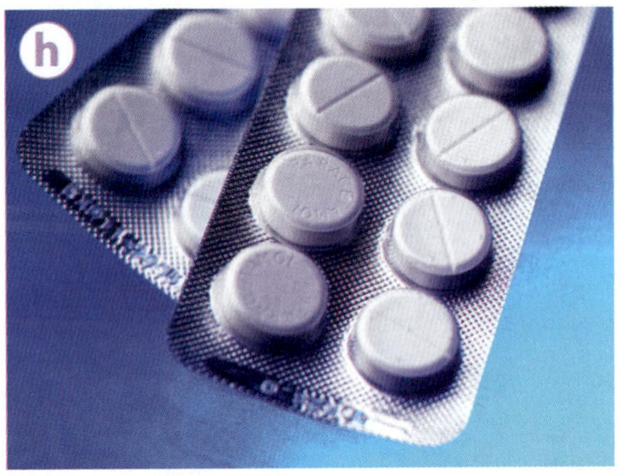
h

i

CD2 13

You already know that we eat the roots, stems and fruit of plants, but did you know that we also eat the seeds? Rice, wheat and corn are all seeds of a plant.

Plants give us the **vitamins** and **minerals** we need to grow and stay healthy. Plants give us the **oxygen** we need to breathe, too.

Wood from trees gives us **heat** and **shelter**, and we also make **paper** from trees. We make **medicine** from plants, too.

1 **Look at photos a–i. What do we need plants for?**

2 Me **Identify objects in your classroom made from plants. Make a list.**

DID YOU KNOW?

Money is made from plants.

A special plant

CD2 14

CD2 15

The **Venus Fly Trap** is a special plant. It makes its own food like all other plants, but it also catches insects and spiders and eats them for extra food. Its leaves have tiny hairs and when an insect walks across a leaf and touches these hairs, the leaves close very quickly. The insect can't escape and the Venus Fly Trap slowly eats it. After about ten days, when the plant has eaten the insect, the leaves open again.

MY SCIENCE PROJECT

MY FAVOURITE TREE

1 Take a photo or draw a picture of your favourite tree.
2 Measure the tree's trunk and do a bark rubbing.
3 Describe the tree's leaves and identify their margins.
4 Write a text about your favourite tree.

REMEMBER!

There's = There is
It's = It is
Here's = Here is

My favourite tree is the oak. There's an oak tree near my house. It's 87cm around its trunk. The trunk is brown and rough. The oak tree is deciduous and it has lobed leaves. Its fruit is the acorn. Here's a photo of the oak tree, and of me doing a bark rubbing on the tree.

6 Habitats — Where living things live

CD2 17

A **habitat** is a specific place where living things live. There are many different types of habitats on Earth. There are habitats in the **Arctic region**, **savannahs**, **deserts**, **tropical rainforests** and **temperate forests**. Each habitat has different **conditions**. These conditions are different because of many reasons including where in the world the habitat is. Habitats can be humid or **dry**, or they can be **hot**, **warm**, **cool** or **cold**. They can have different types of **soil** or **rock**, too. We can also classify habitats into **water** habitats and **land** habitats.

humid *(adj)* when the air feels hot and wet.

1 Identify the habitats a–d.

2 Say the *Habitats* chant.

3 Where do you think the animals in the photos live? Why? Write sentences.

I think camels live in the desert because it's …

4 What do you think are the different conditions in each habitat in photos a–d?

The Arctic region and savannahs

CD2 18

It's very cold in the **Arctic region** and it usually snows. There are no trees, and only a few plants grow in the summer. The Arctic region is a habitat for animals, such as the Arctic fox and polar bears. These animals have thick, white fur to protect them from the cold and for camouflage.

CD2 19

Savannahs are hot and very dry for most of the year. It only rains in savannahs in the summer when it's humid. This means that plants can only grow well in summer, and that it's difficult for animals to find water during the rest of the year.

Savannahs are habitats for animals, such as zebras, giraffes, gazelles and lions.

DID YOU KNOW?

Although the Arctic fox's fur is white, it turns brown in the spring when the snow melts.

1 True or false? Copy the sentences and correct the ones that are false.

a The Arctic region is hot all year.
b In the savannah, it only rains in the summer.
c Plants never grow in the Arctic region.

2 Read and answer the questions.

a Why do you think that some Arctic animals have white fur?
b Do you think that giraffes could live in the Arctic region? Why/why not?

CD2 20

Tropical rainforests are hot and humid. They have a lot of rain, and many different types of trees, bushes and grasses grow there. Tropical rainforests are habitats for animals, such as parrots, monkeys and frogs.

Deserts are hot and dry. Plants, such as cacti grow in the desert. Deserts are habitats for nocturnal animals. Nocturnal animals sleep in the day and are active at night. Scorpions and spiders also live in the desert.

Temperate forests are both warm and cool in summer, and cold in winter. They can have bushes, grasses, and deciduous or evergreen trees. Temperate forests are habitats for animals, such as foxes, rabbits, mice and snails.

1 Copy and complete the sentences.

______ are hot and humid.

______ are both warm and cool in summer or cold in winter.

______ are hot and dry.

2 Why are many desert animals nocturnal?

Water habitats

Living things can live in the **water** and on **land**. There are **saltwater** habitats and **freshwater** habitats.

Oceans and **seas** are saltwater habitats. Many saltwater animals are invertebrates, such as **jellyfish** and **octopus**. There are also many different types of fish and mammals, such as **dolphins** and **whales**, that live in saltwater habitats. Some saltwater animals are herbivores and eat **seaweed** or **plankton**, but others are carnivores.

Rivers and **lakes** are freshwater habitats. The plants and animals that live in and around rivers and lakes interact with each other and their habitat.

The heron catches fish.

Fish eat plants, other animals or both. Some fish even eat dead animals.

Water voles eat roots and live in the soil near lakes and rivers.

1 **How are some animals adapted to a water habitat?**

2 **Copy and complete the sentences.**

oceans and seas   rivers and lakes

________ are freshwater. ________ are saltwater.

Dolphins and whales live in ________.

Mammals, such as water voles, and amphibians, such as frogs, live in ________.

Interaction in ecosystems

CD2 22

A habitat is a specific place where living things live, so what is an **ecosystem**? A group of the same living things that live in the same place at the same time is called a popultion. When these populations interact with each other, they form a **community**. When communities interact with other communities and their surroundings, they form an ecosystem.

An ecosystem is like the town or city where you live. The community is your neighbourhood. The population is your family. Your habitat is your house!

1 **Identify the living things in photos a–h and how they interact with each other.**

2 **Describe the populations, communities and ecosystems of the tropical rainforest habitat, and how the animals interact with each other.**

The food chain

In an ecosystem, living things interact with each other and their habitat to get food. Plants use energy from the Sun to make their own food. Without plants, there would be no life on Earth. We call plants **producers**.

Animals can't make their own food, so they eat plants and other animals. We call animals **consumers**. Consumers can be carnivores, herbivores or omnivores. What type of consumer are you?

When living things die, they provide food for **decomposers**, such as fungi and worms. These decomposers clean the dead material and give nutrients back to the soil. Plants need these nutrients to make their own food, and so the process starts again! This process is called **the food chain**.

In this food chain, the grass is the producer. The rabbit is the consumer because it eats the grass. The fox is also a consumer because the fox eats the rabbit. The fungi are decomposers.

1. **Sing the *Food chain* song.**
2. **Identify the producer, consumers and decomposer in the pictures. Describe the food chain.**
3. **Do you think most habitats have more producers or more consumers?**
4. **What did you eat yesterday? Can you make a food chain?**

Let's investigate! Food chains

Make a food chain.

You need:
- paper plates
- string

How does the food chain work?

a Choose an ecosystem.

b Identify the producers, consumers and decomposers.

c Write about your food chain.

In this food chain, the grass is the producer. The rabbit is a consumer because it eats the grass. The eagle is also a consumer because the eagle eats the rabbit. The fungi are decomposers.

A surprise under the sea

Sharks are fish. They live in oceans and can be as small as twenty centimetres or as long as twelve metres! Most sharks are carnivores and they are at the top of the food chain. This means they don't have any predators. Some sharks are herbivores and eat plankton. Most sharks are oviparous. Sharks are dangerous animals but, in fact, they very rarely attack humans.

MY SCIENCE PROJECT

PROTECTING ECOSYSTEMS

1 **Choose an ecosystem.**
2 **Draw the ecosystem or include a photo.**
3 **Write about some plants and animals that live there.**
4 **Write about the food chain in this ecosystem.**

REMEMBER!

grass → grass**es**
butterfly → butterfl**ies**

It's hot and humid in the tropical rainforest, and it rains a lot. Many different types of plants grow here, such as tall trees and grasses, and flowers with bright colours.

Many animals live here. Monkeys, frogs, snakes, parrots, butterflies and insects can all live in the rainforest. Tropical rainforests have a complex ecosystem. The plants are the producers. The insects eat the plants. The frogs eat the insects, and the snakes eat the frogs!

Learning to learn

1 Copy and complete the word map.

savannahs   freshwater   tropical rainforests   oceans and seas

Habitats

- **Water habitats**

  - saltwater
    - ______
  - ______
    - rivers and lakes

- **Land habitats**

  - deserts
  - ______
  - ______
  - Arctic region
  - temperate forests

2 Use the word map to copy and complete the sentences.

a Some land habitats are the Arctic region, ______, deserts, ______ and ______.

b Oceans and seas are ______ habitats.

c ______ and ______ are freshwater habitats.

3 **What are the conditions in these habitats? Copy and complete the chart. Write *yes* or *no*.**

	Deserts	Savannahs	Temperate forests	Tropical rainforests	Arctic region
Hot					
Warm/cool					
Cold					

4 **Identify the producer, consumers and decomposer. Order and copy the food chain.**

a 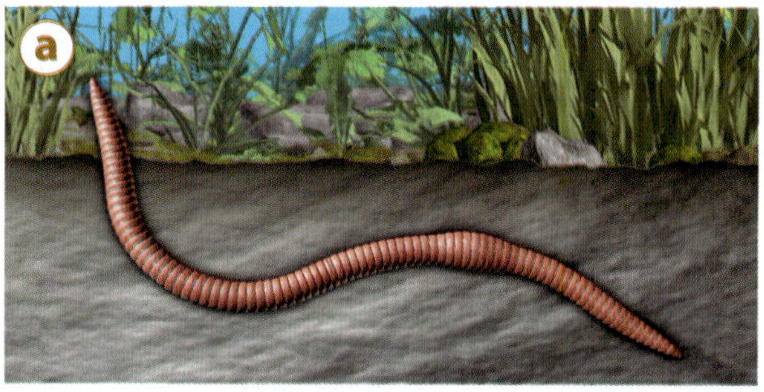

worm

b 

lion

c 

zebra

d 

grass

5 **Copy and complete the sentences about the food chain.**

The grass is a ______. The zebra is a ______.

The lion is a ______. The worm is a ______.

I can describe different habitats. ☆ ☆ ☆

I know about interaction in ecosystems. ☆ ☆ ☆

I can describe food chains. ☆ ☆ ☆

7 Water and air on Earth

Where we find water

In this unit we're going to learn about air and water on Earth.

All living things need this. We can't see it, but it's all around us. What is it?

All living things need **water** and **air** to live.

Water is found in many places in and around the Earth. It's found in three **states**. These are **solid**, **liquid** and **gas**. Most of the water on Earth is **saltwater**, and only a little is **freshwater**. **Oceans** and **seas** are saltwater. **Rivers**, **lakes**, **icecaps** and **groundwater**, which is water below the Earth, are freshwater. **Reservoirs** are man-made lakes for storing freshwater.

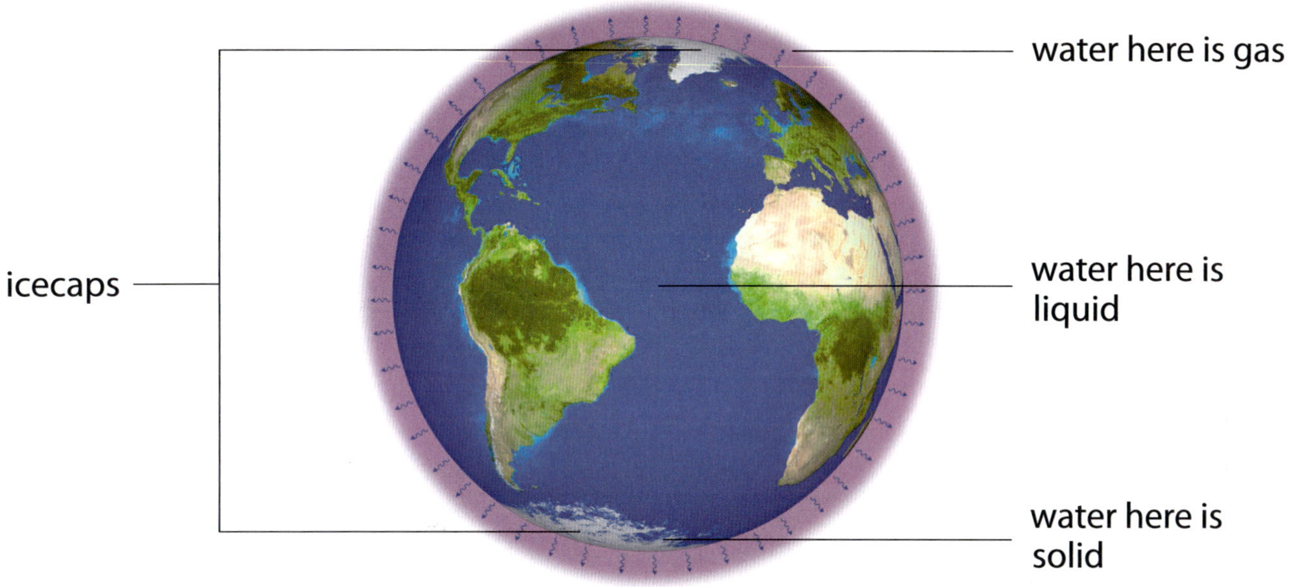

Plants can't grow without air. People and animals can't breathe without air. Air is found mainly in the **atmosphere**, which is the layer of gases that surround the Earth.

DID YOU KNOW?

Nearly three-quarters of the Earth's fresh water is frozen at the South Pole.

1 **Say the *Water* chant.**

2 **Identify the different forms of water in photos a–g.**

3 **Copy and complete the chart.**

freshwater	saltwater

4 **Choose the correct word and write the sentence.**

Most of the water on Earth is **saltwater** / **freshwater**.

5 **What's the difference between lakes and reservoirs?**

6 **Where is air mainly found on Earth?**

Characteristics of air

Air is all around us but we can't see it. Air is a **mixture of gases**, but it consists mainly of oxygen and nitrogen. Air and water have the same characteristics; they have no smell, no taste and no colour.

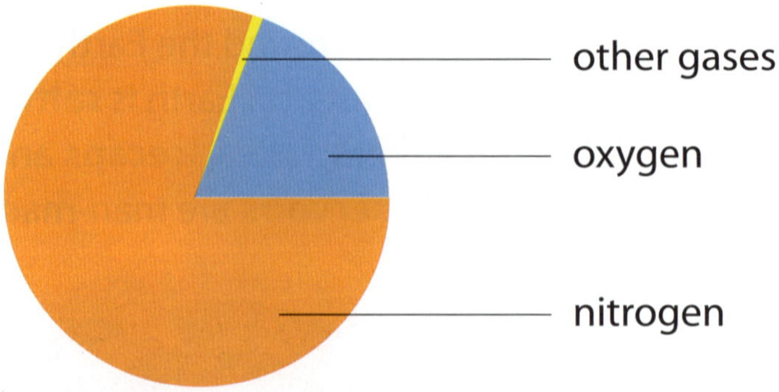

Let's investigate! More characteristics of air

Investigate whether air has weight.

You need:
- 2 balloons
- 3 pieces of string
- a ruler
- a pin

a Blow up two balloons.
b Tie them to the ends of a ruler.
c Hang the ruler.
d Make sure the balloons are balanced.
e Burst one balloon with a pin.
f What happens? Why?
g Result: Does air have weight?

1 **Does air weigh more than water?** 2 **How can you investigate this?**

Wind

Wind is moving air. Hot air goes up, and cold air goes down. The difference in air temperature causes wind, which moves air from one place to another. This is why clouds move.

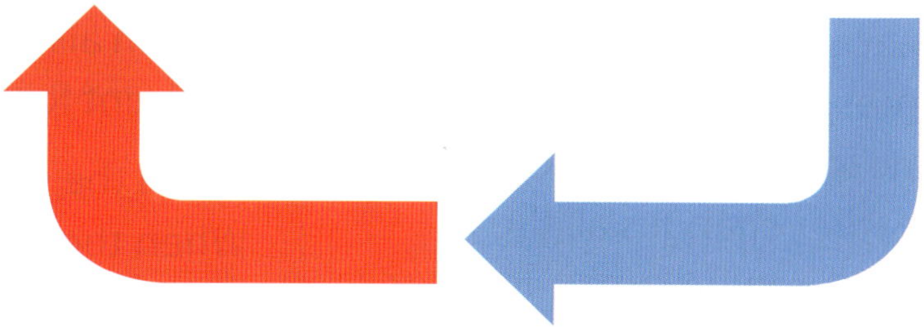

There are different types of wind. When there is no wind or we can't feel any wind, we say that it is **calm**. A little wind is called a **breeze**. A breeze moves the leaves on the trees. It can help us feel cooler on a hot day. A **gale** is a strong wind. A gale moves the branches on trees and can sometimes blow trees down! A **hurricane** is a very strong wind. A hurricane can destroy houses and other buildings. Is there any wind where you are today? Can you identify the type of wind?

calm

breeze

gale

hurricane

We can measure how fast the wind is moving with an **anemometer**. We can find out the direction the wind is blowing with a **weather vane**.

anemometer

weather vane

1 What is wind? Write your answer.

Wind is ...

2 Copy and order the wind strengths.

gale breeze hurricane

3 Match and write the sentences.

a An anemometer tells us — wind direction.
b A weather vane tells us — wind speed.

Weather

CD2 35

Weather is the state of the atmosphere at a certain time in a certain place. Weather changes all the time. It can be **sunny** in the morning, **raining** in the afternoon and **windy** at night. What's the weather like now where you are today?

CD2 36

We can also experience different **temperatures** and different forms of **precipitation**, too.

When the weather is **hot**, the temperature is high. When the weather is **cold**, the temperature is low.

Precipitation is water falling from the atmosphere to the ground. There are different types of precipitation. Precipitation can be liquid, such as **rain** or solid, such as **snow**. When balls of ice fall from the atmosphere, we call this form of precipitation **hail**.

1 CD2 37 **Say the *Weather* rap.**

2 **What is weather?**

3 **What types of weather can we experience?**

4 **What is the difference between rain and hail?**

5 **Look at the weather map.**

a Which place has the highest temperature?

b Where is there precipitation?

c What season do you think it is?

CD2 38

We can measure **wind speed** with an **anemometer**, **rainfall** with a **rain gauge** and **temperature** with a **thermometer**. What are the children in these photos measuring?

Investigate and measure the weather where you are.

You need:

- a thermometer
- plasticine

You need:

- 4 small paper or plastic cups
- a pencil with a rubber on the end
- 2 pieces of cardboard
- glue
- a pin
- plasticine

You need:

- a plastic bottle
- scissors

a Measure the wind speed, rainfall and temperature for one week. Write what the weather's like each day.

b Which days had the strongest winds, the most rainfall and the highest temperature?

c What was the weather like on these days? Can you think why?

Freshwater

CD2 39

You already know the places on Earth where we can find freshwater, but did you know that we can't drink all this water?

We can only drink clean freshwater. We call this water **drinking water**. Water from rivers and lakes is **non-drinking water**.

There are more and more people on Earth who need freshwater, so we must save water. How do you use freshwater every day?

DID YOU KNOW?

Freshwater is rare. Only 3% of all the water on Earth is freshwater.

DID YOU KNOW?

We can survive without food for about a month, but we can only survive for about a week without water.

1 **How do you use freshwater every day?**

2 **Can we drink all freshwater?**

3 **Why must we save water?**

4 **How can you save water?**

5 **Do you think there is enough drinking water for everyone on Earth?**

The water cycle

CD2 40

Water on Earth is always changing state and place. This is known as the **water cycle**.

When the Sun heats water, water vapour rises. This is **evaporation**. When the water vapour cools, it turns into water drops and forms **clouds**. This is **condensation**. The wind moves the clouds. When the clouds cool, water from the clouds falls as rain. If it is very cold, the water freezes and falls as **snow**. Rain and snow are both types of **precipitation**. The water that falls to the ground eventually goes into rivers. It can travel to the rivers across the surface of the Earth or underground. Rivers take the water back to the ocean and seas. This is called **collection**. Now the cycle begins again.

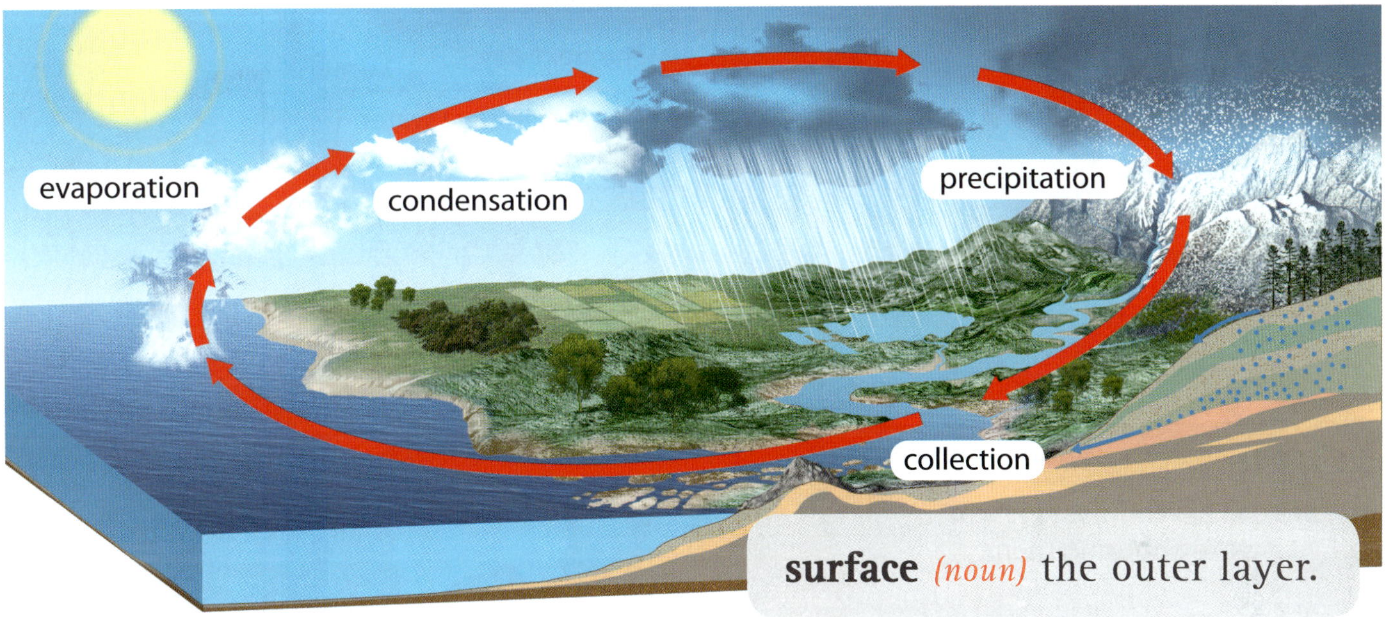

surface *(noun)* the outer layer.

1 What is the water cycle? Write your answer.

The water cycle is ...

2 Order and copy the sentences about the water cycle.

- Precipitation eventually goes into rivers and back to the sea.
- The wind moves the clouds, and the water drops fall as precipitation.
- Now the cycle begins again.
- It turns into water drops and forms clouds.
- When the Sun heats water, water vapour rises.

How can you save water by only watering plants early in the morning or at night?

The drought

CD2 41

CD2 42

A **drought** can happen if it doesn't rain for a long period of time. Although droughts usually happen in summer, little precipitation in winter can mean that there's not enough water in reservoirs for the dry summer months. During a drought, rivers can be dry, and it's difficult for plants and fish to survive. We all need to save water.

MY SCIENCE PROJECT

HOW I USE AND SAVE WATER

1 Make a list of how you use water and how you can save water.

2 Draw pictures or take photos of how you use and save water.

3 Write a text to describe how you use and save water.

REMEMBER!

always ✓✓✓
usually ✓✓
sometimes ✓
never ✗

We all use water every day. I use water in the bathroom to have a shower, wash my hands and face, and brush my teeth. I always turn off the tap!

I also drink lots of water to stay healthy. I sometimes drink six glasses of water every day!

Learning to learn

1 Copy and complete the word maps.

reservoirs drinking water atmosphere saltwater groundwater no smell

Air and water

- [ ]
- no colour
- no taste
- weight

Air – [ ]

Water

- oceans and seas
- rivers and lakes
- [ ]
- icecaps
- [ ]

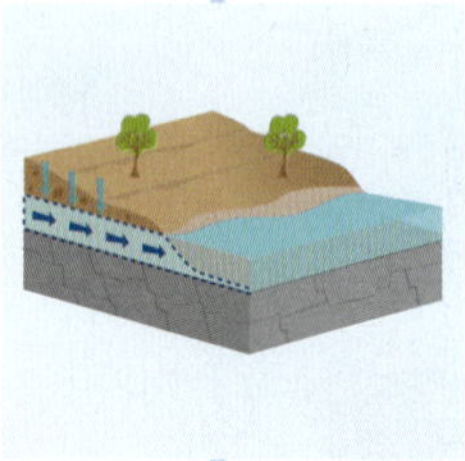

[ ]

freshwater – [ ]

2 True or false? Copy the sentences and correct the ones that are false.

a Oceans and seas are freshwater.

b Air and water have weight.

c Icecaps and reservoirs are saltwater.

d We can drink all freshwater.

3 Order the wind speeds from the lightest to the strongest.

calm

hurricane

breeze

gale

4 Copy and complete the sentences.

liquid saltwater air atmosphere

All living things need water and ______ to live.

Air is found mainly in the ______.

Water has three states: solid, ______ and gas.

Most of the water on Earth is ______, and only a little is freshwater.

5 Match, order and write the water cycle process.

The clouds cool, and water from the clouds falls as rain or snow.	collection
Water vapour cools and forms clouds.	evaporation
Precipitation falls to the ground and travels to the oceans and seas.	condensation
The Sun heats water, and water vapour rises.	precipitation

I know where we find water and air. ☆ ☆ ☆

I know some characteristics of water and air. ☆ ☆ ☆

I can identify different weather conditions. ☆ ☆ ☆

I know that freshwater is rare. ☆ ☆ ☆

I can describe the water cycle. ☆ ☆ ☆

8 Landscapes

Different landscapes

In this unit we're going to learn about different landscapes around us and how they can change. We're also going to discover more about life in these landscapes. What can you see when you look out of the window?

A landscape is everything we can see in an area. There are many different land forms in a landscape. They can be high, low, big or small. All these different land forms are called **relief**.

A **mountain landscape** has **mountains** and **valleys**.

A **flat landscape** has **plains** and **plateaus**.

A **coastal landscape** has **beaches** and **cliffs**.

1 **Say the *Landscapes* chants.**

2 **Copy and complete the sentences.**

a A mountain landscape has ______ .

b A flat landscape has ______ .

c A coastal landscape has ______ .

3 **What natural and man-made features can you see in the different landscapes?**

4 **Copy and complete the chart.**

Landscapes	
Natural features	Man-made features

5 **Listen to the children talking about the landscapes where they live.**

There are **natural** and **man-made** features in a landscape.

Natural features have not been changed by people. Mountains, forests, plateaus and cliffs are some natural features.

Man-made features of a landscape are made by people. Fields, villages, roads and bridges are some man-made features.

Are valleys, railways, rivers, forests, buildings, plains and ports natural or man-made features?

Mountain landscapes

CD2 48

A group of mountains is called a **mountain range**. Mountains are very high, but **hills** are lower. **Valleys** are the area of low land between mountains and hills. We can often find rivers flowing through valleys. The land near rivers in valleys is fertile, so plants grow well here.

Roads in a mountain landscape are narrow and winding, so it's difficult to travel. There are only small towns and villages in the mountains.

CD2 49

The top of a mountain is called the **summit**. Very few plants and animals can live at the summit. The sides of a mountain are called **slopes**. The bottom of a mountain is called the **foot**.

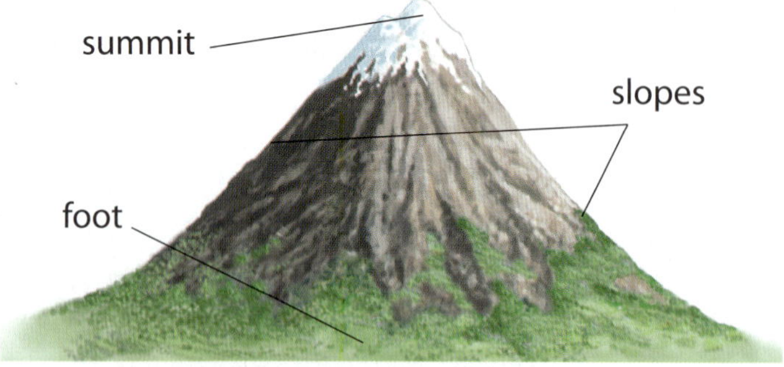

DID YOU KNOW?

The highest mountain in Spain is Teide. It's a volcano.

fertile *(adj)* land where plants can grow well.

1 **Read and answer the questions.**

a What is a group of mountains called?

b Which is higher, a hill or a mountain?

c What are valleys?

2 **Choose the correct words and write the sentences.**

a Mountain life is **easy** / **hard**.

b Very **few** / **many** plants and animals live at the top of a mountain.

c Mountain roads are **wide** / **narrow**.

d Mountain towns are **big** / **small**.

3 **Copy and label the picture of a mountain.**

4 CD2 50 **Listen and learn about life in the mountains.**

There are no mountains or hills in a flat landscape, but we can see **plains** and **plateaus**. A **plain** is a large area of flat land. Plains are low. A **plateau** is a high plain with steep sides. The biggest plateau in Spain is La Meseta.

A flat landscape is a good place for growing **crops**. Farmers grow crops on plains. Wheat and rice are two important crops in Spain. We use wheat to make bread.

Many people live in a flat landscape. There are big towns and cities, and there are wide, straight roads. There are railways, too.

1 True or false? Copy the sentences and correct the ones that are false.

a Flat landscapes have hills.

b Plateaus have steep sides.

c Plains are higher than plateaus.

2 What's the difference between a plain and a plateau?

3 Why do you think farmers plant crops on plains?

4 Listen and learn about life on the plains.

Relief maps

CD2 56

This is a **relief map**. It shows the landscape in different colours to represent different relief. The key tells us what each colour means.

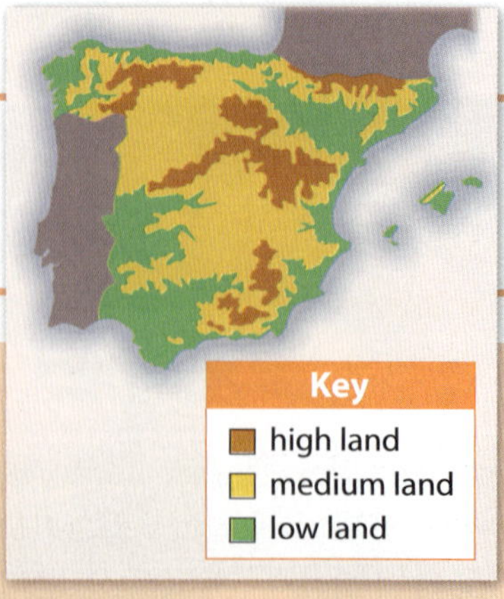

1 What colour are these features on the relief map?

- mountains
- hills and plateaus
- plains

2 Match the landscapes to the correct relief maps.

Let's investigate! Relief maps

Investigate relief maps.

You need:

- brown, yellow and green plasticine
- sticks
- pieces of paper

First, use the green plasticine to show low land. **Valleys** and **plains** are low land.

Next, use the yellow plasticine to show medium land. **Hills** and **plateaus** are medium land.

Then use the brown plasticine to show high land. **Mountains** are high land.

Finally, label your relief map using the sticks and paper.

Rivers

Rivers can be long or short, but they are all made up of three main parts. These parts are called the **upper course**, the **middle course** and the **lower course**. Most rivers begin in hills or mountains.

The place where a river begins is called the **source**. When a river leaves its source, it becomes wider and forms bends called **meanders**. Small rivers that join the main river are called **tributaries**. A river ends its journey at the mouth. The **mouth** is where a river meets the sea, ocean or a lake.

Rivers are filled with freshwater and give life to the land. What rivers are near you?

source

tributaries

meanders

mouth

1 **Say the *River* chant.**

2 **Identify the features in the river picture.**

3 **Where do you think the river is fastest? Why?**

Coastal landscapes

CD2 59

A coastal landscape is by the sea.

A **beach** is an area of low, flat land next to the sea. Beaches have sand or rocks.

A **cliff** is a high wall of rock next to the sea.

A **bay** is where the sea goes into the land.

A **cape** is an area of land that goes into the sea.

An **island** is an area of land that is surrounded by water.

A group of islands is called an **archipelago**.

1 CD2 60 CD2 61 CD2 62 **Say the *Coastal landscapes* chants and rap.**

2 **Copy and label the features of a coastal landscape.**

3 **Order and write the letters to find features of a coastal landscape.**

sdialn hcaeb pace

fcilf aby elpaaoghcri

Coastal landscapes change

CD2 63

Most towns on the coast were originally small **fishing villages**. People go on holiday to the coast, and now many of these villages are very big. Today they are **tourist resorts** where there are new hotels, apartments, shops and restaurants. There are **marinas** full of boats.

CD2 64

Protecting coastal landscapes

CD2 65

Many plants and animals live in the sea and on beaches and cliffs. We must respect them when we go to the coast. Don't pick wild flowers. Don't climb the cliffs because you could fall or destroy the animals' homes. If you pick up animals, always put them back in the same place. Be careful because some animals can hurt you! Never drop litter or leave bottles. They can hurt animals or people.

1 **How do coastal landscapes change?**

2 CD2 64 **Listen and learn about life in a coastal town.**

3 **Who isn't respecting the coastal landscape? Why?**

4 **What can we do to protect coastal landscapes?**

A trip down the river

CD2 67

The river Nile is in Africa. It flows through nine countries to the Mediterranean Sea. It's the longest river in the world!

The Nile is home to many different animals including the Nile crocodile. The Nile crocodile eats mainly fish, but it can also attack large animals, even zebras! Although the Nile crocodile is a dangerous predator, it is also a caring parent. The mother and father crocodiles guard their eggs until they hatch.

My Science Presentation

MY LOCAL AREA

1. **Collect information from the internet, tourist information office or other reference sources and write about your local area.**
2. **Find out:**
   - a The name of the nearest city and some towns and villages.
   - b What the weather is like at different times of the year.
   - c What the landscape is like.
   - d The names of local rivers.
   - e What plants and animals live in the area.
3. **Write a text using your information.**
4. **Find photos, postcards or draw pictures to go with your text.**
5. **Use your text and your pictures to make a poster.**
6. **Present your poster to the class.**

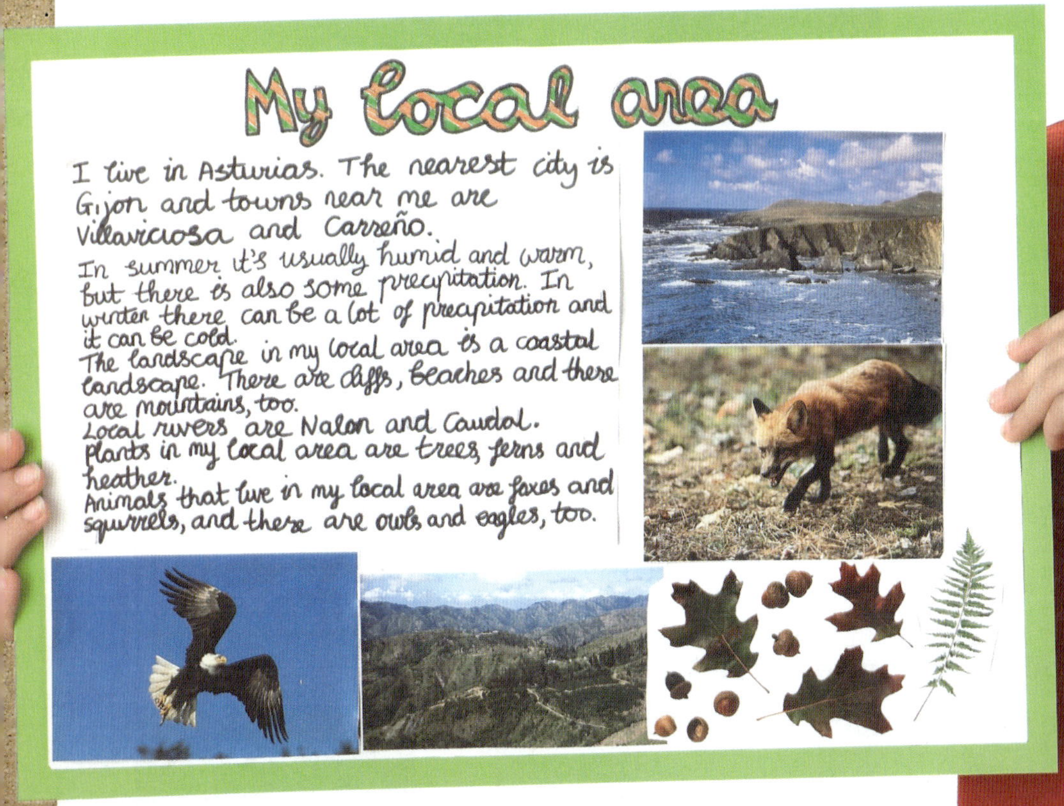

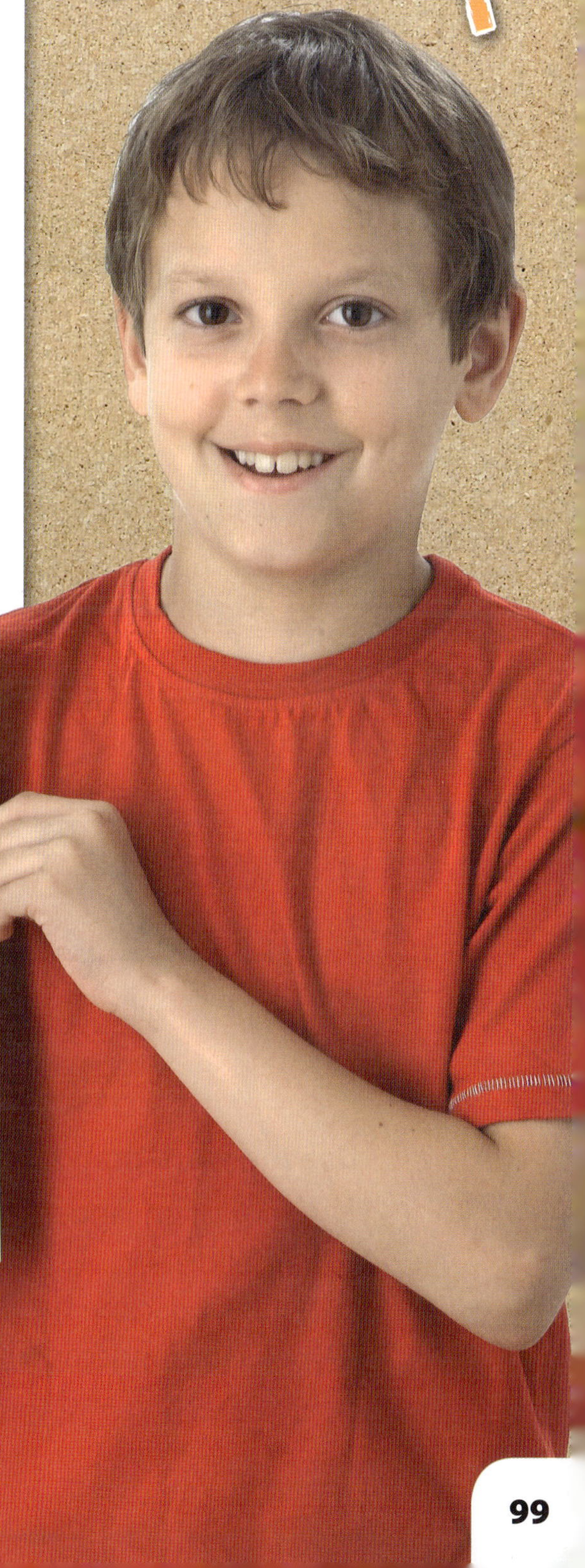

Learning to learn

1 Copy and complete the word map. cliffs valleys plains bays

Landscapes

Mountain landscape

mountains

______

hills

Flat landscape

______

plateaus

Coastal landscape

beaches

______

islands

______

capes

2 Use the word map to copy and complete the sentences.

a A mountain landscape has mountains, ______ and hills.

b A flat landscape has ______ and plateaus.

c A coastal landscape has beaches, ______ , islands, ______ and capes.

3 **Copy and classify these features of a landscape.**

mountain
town
plain
valley
port
bridge
cliff
road

Natural features

Man-made features

4 **Copy and complete the sentences about the parts of a river.**

- **a** Small rivers that join a main river are called ______ .
- **b** The place where a river ends its journey is called the ______ .
- **c** The place where a river begins its journey is called the ______ .
- **d** ______ are when a river becomes wider and forms bends.

5 **Copy and match the landscapes with the sentences.**

- a mountain landscape
- a flat landscape
- a coastal landscape

- Tourists go to the beach here in summer.
- There are summits.
- There's a marina.
- Roads are narrow and winding.
- Farmers grow crops like wheat and rice.
- There are big towns and cities.

I know about different landscapes. ☆ ☆ ☆

I can identify natural and man-made features of landscapes. ☆ ☆ ☆

I know about life in different landscapes. ☆ ☆ ☆

I can identify the parts of a river. ☆ ☆ ☆

I know how landscapes change. ☆ ☆ ☆

Units 5–8 review

CD2 68

SCIENCE CLUB QUIZ

1 What is the reproductive organ of a plant?

2 What is the difference between a deciduous tree and an evergreen tree?

3 Why do few plants grow in the Arctic region?

4 What are the conditions in savannahs?

5 What is a food chain made up of?

6 What is wind?

7 What are the characteristics of air and water?

8 What are the four processes of the water cycle?

9 What is the difference between mountains and hills?

10 What are the three courses of a river?

CD2 69 Listen and check your answers.

How did you do?

8–10 points	5–7 points	0–4 points
Excellent	Good	Try again

SCIENCE CHALLENGE

Find a friend. Decide who is Pupil A and who is Pupil B. Take it in turns to ask and answer the questions in the Science Challenge.

PUPIL A

1. *These protect the flower before it opens.*
2. *These have pollen at their ends.*
3. *These parts of a plant absorb water and the minerals that the plants need to grow. They fix the plant in the ground.*
4. *These parts of a plant use sunlight to help make their own food.*
5. *This ecosystem is warm in summer and cold in winter.*
6. *This is formed when different populations interact with each other.*
7. *This is a man-made lake for storing freshwater.*
8. *This is the strongest type of wind.*
9. *This is a large area of flat land.*
10. *This is an area of land that goes into the sea.*

PUPIL B

1. *These can be many different colours and attract insects to the flower.*
2. *This is the part of the flower where the seeds develop.*
3. *These parts of a plant carry water and minerals from the roots to the rest of the plant. They support the plant.*
4. *This ecosystem is hot and humid.*
5. *This is a group of the same living things that live in the same place at the same time.*
6. *This is a natural freshwater feature we find underground.*
7. *This is a light wind.*
8. *This is a strong wind.*
9. *This is a high plain with steep sides.*
10. *This is an area of land surrounded by water.*

Can you remember the definitions of these words?

thorn *(noun)* ...
pollen *(noun)* ...
germinate *(verb)* ...
humid *(adj)* ...
surface *(noun)* ...
fertile *(adj)* ...

9 The top layer of Earth — Soil

You already know that all living things need food, water and air, but **soil** is important, too.

So, what is soil? Soil is made up of particles of **rocks** and **minerals**, **air**, **water** and **humus**, which is the remains of dead plants and animals. Many different types of animals live in the soil and every single one of these animals is important. **Decomposers** in the soil help to turn the dead plants and animals into humus. Humus contains the **nutrients** that plants need to grow.

We can find soil on the top layer of the Earth.

Trees need soil to live and grow.

1 Say the *Soil* chant.

2 Listen to Clara, Nico and Professor Eco talking about living things in the soil.

3 Examine a sample of soil and describe your observations.

a What colour is it?
b How does it feel?
c Can you see any small rocks?
d Can you see any living things?

4 What is soil made up of?

5 What is humus?

6 Why are animals important to soil?

7 Where can we find soil?

Soil layers

Soil is made up of different **layers**. The top layer is called **topsoil**. This soft layer contains roots, insects and other tiny living things, such as bacteria and fungi, which are called **decomposers**. There is water and air in topsoil, too. Topsoil has lots of humus and is the most productive layer of soil.

The middle layer is called **subsoil**. This layer has less water and air, very little humus, some small rocks, and the soil is hard.

The bottom layer is called **bedrock**. This layer is very hard and is made up of bigger rocks. Bedrock has very little water and air.

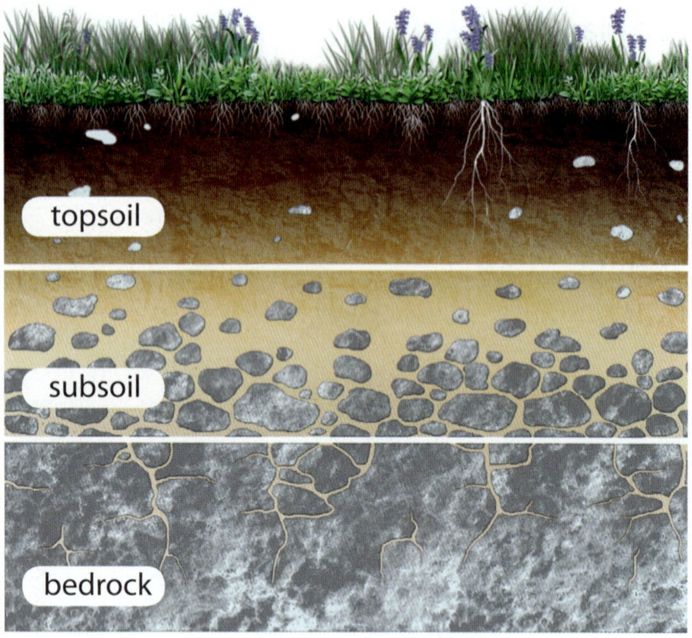

Let's investigate! Soil layers

Observe, identify and describe soil layers.

How do soil layers form?

You need:

- a jar with a lid
- water
- soil

a Fill half a jar with water and add the soil.

b Put the lid on the jar and shake it.

c When the soil settles, what can you see?

1 **What are the three layers of soil?**

2 **Say the *Soil* rap.**

3 **Copy and complete the chart.**

bigger rocks insects less water and air
small rocks decomposers little water and air

Topsoil	Subsoil	Bedrock

Types of soil

There are lots of different types of soil. We can classify soil by the quantity of humus and water it contains. Soil can be **fertile**, **poor** or **arid**. Soil can also be different colours: black, red, yellow, white, brown or grey. The colour of soil can tell us a lot about it. If soil is dark, this usually means that it has lots of humus.

Fertile soil has lots of humus and water. Many plants can grow well in this type of soil. There is fertile soil in deciduous temperate forests.

Poor soil has little humus and water. It has more rocks than fertile soil. Only hardy plants, such as olive trees can grow in poor soil. There is poor soil in savannahs.

Arid soil has very little humus and water. It has lots of rocks or sand. Only very hardy plants, such as cacti can grow in arid soil. There is arid soil in deserts.

hardy *(adj)* resistant, strong.

1 **What are the three types of soil? Describe their characteristics.**
2 **Why is there lots of humus in the soil in deciduous temperate forests?**
3 **What type of soil is there where you live?**

The soil ecosystem

This is a soil ecosystem. The plants and animals that live in the soil interact with each other.

CD3 9

1 Animals eat plants that grow in the soil.

2 Slugs and snails eat dead plants and animals. Birds and hedgehogs eat the slugs and snails.

3 Plant and animal remains and excrement turn into humus with the help of decomposers in the soil.

4 **Tunnels** made by worms and other animals allow air and water into the soil.

5 Animals shelter in the soil.

1 **How are the living things in the picture interacting with each other in the ecosystem?**

2 **Copy and complete the sentences.**

humus ecosystem snails Decomposers

a Plants and animals are important to the soil ______ .

b Animals, such as ______ eat dead plants and animals.

c ______ living in the soil help turn plant and animal remains into ______ .

DID YOU KNOW?

Worms don't have lungs. They breathe through their skin. Worms have five hearts!

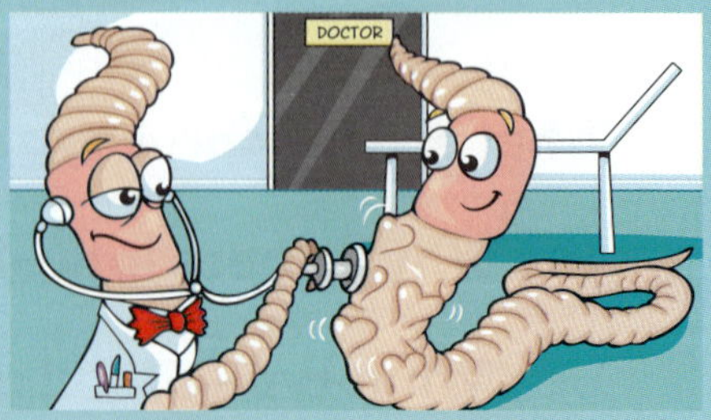

Rocks and minerals

CD3 10

Rocks make up the solid part of the Earth. **Minerals** are the materials rocks are made of. Rocks and minerals are all around us. They are natural non-living things.

Minerals from the Earth are used to make lots of everyday things. We even eat some minerals. Without minerals, there wouldn't be cars or computers. You couldn't brush your teeth because there would be no toothpaste!

Some minerals are very rare and we use them to make jewellery. Can you think of any minerals that are used to make jewellery?

rare *(adj)* difficult to find.

slate

granite

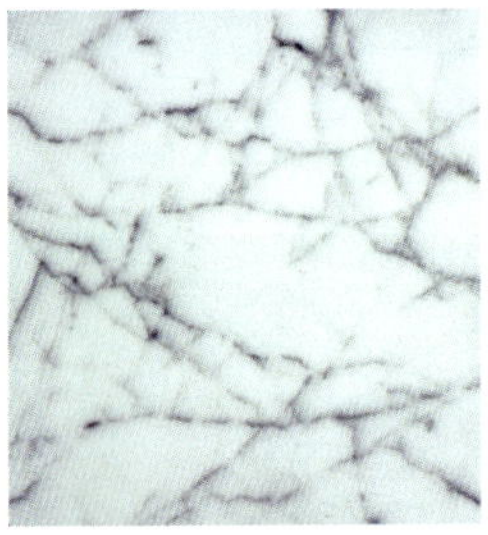

marble

gold

salt

copper

1 **Look at the photos. Find objects made from these rocks and minerals in the kitchen.**

2 **Why do you think rocks and minerals are used to make these objects?**

3 Me **Identify rocks and minerals in your classroom.**

An amazing discovery

CD3 12

CD3 13

When a living thing dies, it can sometimes be buried and preserved by different types of rocks and soil, and a **fossil** is formed. Fossils are the preserved remains of animals or plants that lived on Earth a long time ago. There are lots of different fossils, including fossils of bones, shells and footprints. Fossils can tell us a lot about life on Earth a very long time ago.

The fossil of what scientists think is the biggest dinosaur in Europe was discovered in Spain. This dinosaur, now called *Turiasaurus riodevensis*, was over 35 metres long and weighed the same as seven elephants!

THE SOIL WHERE I LIVE

1 **Observe the soil near you and describe it.**
  a Is it fertile, poor or arid soil?
  b What plants grow in this soil?
  c What animals interact with this soil?

2 **Take photos or draw pictures of what you see.**

3 **Write about the soil near you.**

REMEMBER!

The soil *where* I live is ...

Rabbits eat the grass *which* grows ...

The soil where I live is fertile. This means that plants can grow well.

Farmers grow crops, such as wheat, near where I live. There are lots of brightly coloured flowers in my garden, too. My favourite flower is the crocus which grows in spring.

I sometimes see animals in my garden. Rabbits eat the grass which grows in the soil and worms make tunnels in the soil, which lets air in.

Learning to learn

1 Copy and complete the word map. fertile minerals subsoil humus

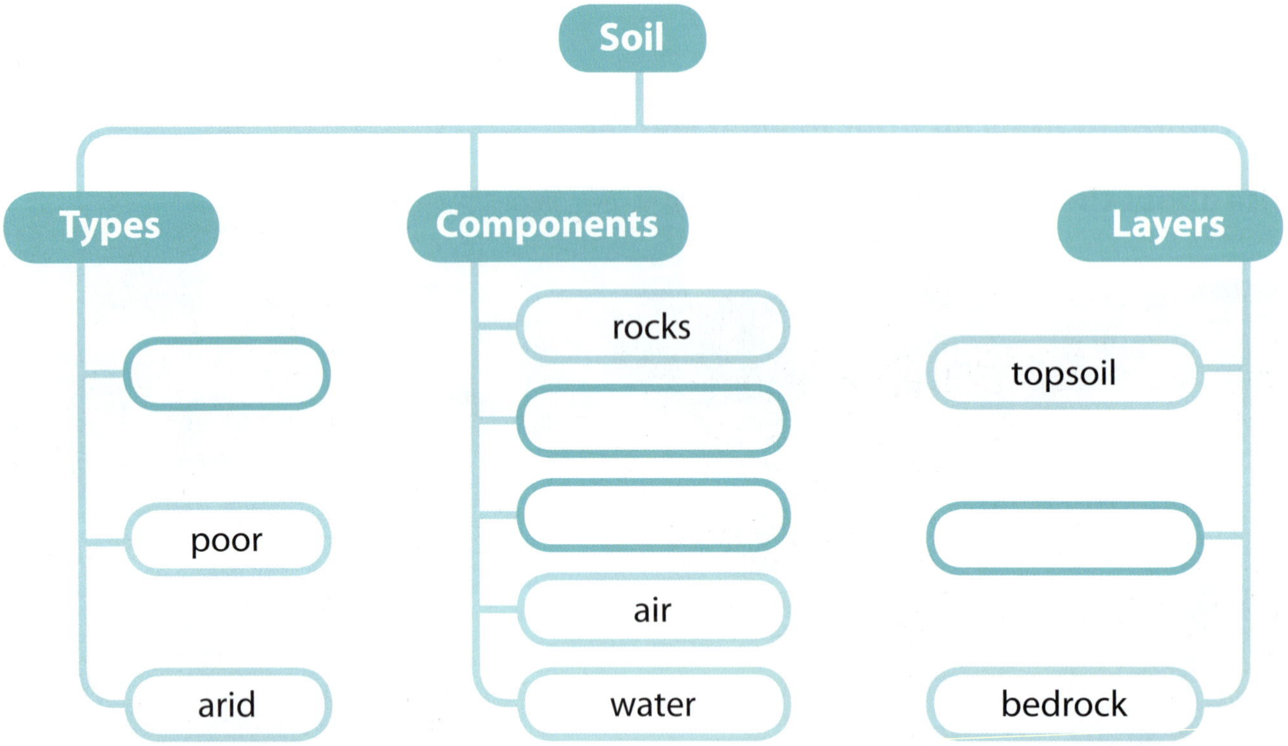

2 Use the word map to copy and complete the sentences.

a Soil can be fertile, ______ or ______ .

b Soil is made up of rocks, minerals, ______ , ______ and ______ .

c There are three layers in the soil. The top layer is called ______ , the middle layer is called ______ and the bottom layer is called ______ .

3 Match and write the sentences.

a Fertile soil has — very little humus and water.
b Poor soil has — lots of humus and water.
c Arid soil has — a little humus and water.

4 In which type of soil do plants grow best? Why? Copy and complete the sentence with your answer.

Plants grow best in ... soil because ...

5 Copy and label the diagram of the soil.

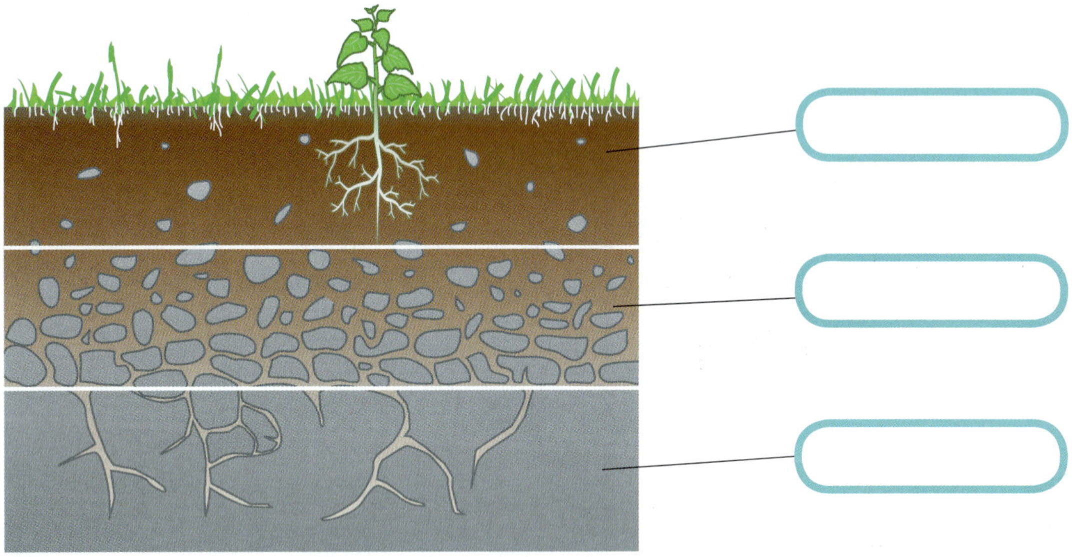

6 Copy and complete the chart. Write the names of two types of rocks and minerals. How do we use them?

Rocks and minerals	Uses

I can recognise the different soil layers. ☆ ☆ ☆

I can identify different types of soil. ☆ ☆ ☆

I can talk about the soil ecosystem. ☆ ☆ ☆

I know how we can use some rocks and minerals. ☆ ☆ ☆

10 Transport and communication

Transport

In this unit we're going to learn about transport and communication.

This vehicle is a form of public transport. It travels underground. Look at the photos. Which form of transport is it?

a

b

c

d

e

f

CD3 14

We use different forms of transport to travel from one place to another and to transport goods. Different vehicles provide us with different forms of transport. We can classify these vehicles by where they travel.

- **Planes** and **helicopters** are forms of **air** travel.
- **Ferries** and **cargo ships** travel by **sea**.
- **Cars**, **trains**, **buses**, **lorries**, **motorbikes**, **vans** and **bicycles** travel on **land**.
- **Metro trains** usually travel **underground**.

You already know that some vehicles are for **people** and that some vehicles are for **goods**. Can you remember which vehicles are for goods?

1 CD3 15 **Say the *Transport* chant.**

2 **Copy and complete the chart to classify the vehicles in the photos.**

Land	Sea	Air

3 Me **What forms of transport do you use?**

Land transport

There are many different types of **land transport**. These vehicles usually have wheels. They travel by **road** or **rail**.

Land vehicles help us travel from one place to another, and we can use them to travel short or long distances.

A disadvantage of land transport is that it can cause **noise pollution** and **air pollution**.

Let's investigate! Forms of land transport

Do a survey of how you travel to school.

What's the most common form of transport in your class?

Make a graph to display your results.

1. **What common feature does land transport usually have?**
2. **What do you think is the most common form of land transport?**
3. **Choose the best form of land transport to:**
   a move house b go shopping c go out with friends to the cinema
4. **What is the fastest form of land transport?**
5. **Which form of land transport doesn't cause noise and air pollution?**

Air and sea transport

CD3 18

Planes and **helicopters** are forms of **air transport**. We use planes when we want to travel long distances and visit other countries. Travelling by plane is the fastest form of transport. A helicopter isn't as fast as a plane, but helicopters can land in difficult places.

Ferries, **ocean liners** and **cargo ships** are forms of **sea transport**. They travel long distances, but they aren't as fast as planes. Ferries and ocean liners carry people, and cargo ships carry goods.

Private and public transport

CD3 19

We can also classify forms of transport into **private transport** and **public transport**. Using private transport means that we can travel where and when we want.

Buses, **trains** and **taxis** are forms of public transport. It's important to try and use public transport as much as possible. If we do this, we can reduce air pollution.

1 **What different forms of air and sea transport can you think of?**

2 **Is a plane or a helicopter better for rescuing people in danger? Why?**

3 **What are the advantages and disadvantages of using private transport?**

4 Me **What forms of public transport are there where you live?**

5 Me **How do you think you can use public transport more?**

6 **Look at the photo on the right. Do you think using public transport is easy or difficult for this person? Why?**

Personal communication

People have always used different forms of **communication**. We communicate with each other every day. We communicate to make friends, to share ideas or feelings, to send or receive information and to learn things.

We use **personal communication** to communicate with another person. Forms of personal communication include the **telephone**, **email**, the **postal service** and, of course, **face-to-face** communication.

We use **landline** telephones and **mobile** telephones. We can use mobile telephones to send **text messages**, to sometimes send **emails** and to look for information on the internet. Sending an email is much quicker than sending a letter. To send an email we must be connected to the internet.

We use the postal service to send **letters**, **postcards** and **parcels** to people. Letters are an old form of communication.

DID YOU KNOW?

The mothers of Roman soldiers sent them letters and parcels when they were far from home to cheer them up!

1 **Identify the forms of personal communication in photos a–d.**

2 Me **What forms of personal communication do you use to:**
- a invite a friend to a party?
- b tell a friend about a problem you have?
- c talk with a member of your family?
- d send a short message quickly?
- e tell a long story?

3 **How is a mobile telephone different to a landline telephone?**

4 **Why do you think it's sometimes better to use face-to-face communication?**

Mass communication

CD3 24

The most important forms of **mass communication** are **newspapers**, **magazines**, **television**, **radio**, and the **internet**. These forms of mass communication are used to send information to lots of people.

a

b

c

d

e

CD3 25

How television news is made

1 Journalists and cameramen record and film important events and send the information to editors.

2 An editor checks and prepares the information for the newsreader.

3 The newsreader reads the news in a studio.

4 Television cameras film the news.

5 A transmitter sends signals to our televisions.

6 Our televisions receive this information and we can watch the news.

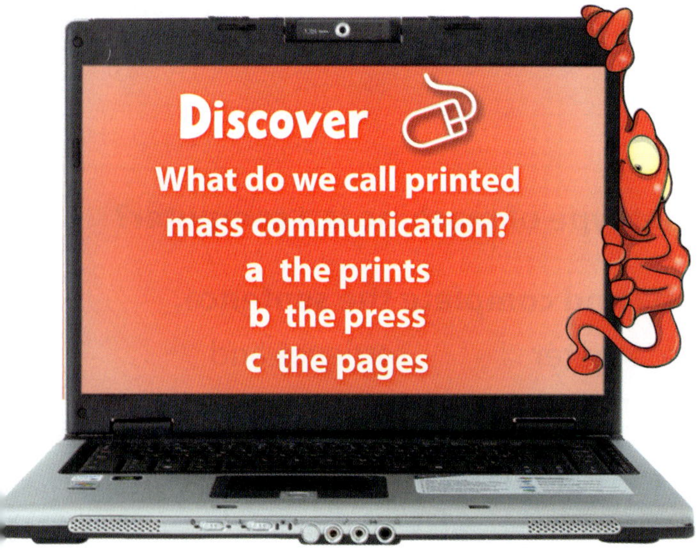

Discover

What do we call printed mass communication?

a the prints
b the press
c the pages

1 **Identify the forms of mass communication in photos a–e.**

2 **What's the difference between personal communication and mass communication?**

The difference between personal communication and mass communication is ...

3 CD3 26 **Say the *Let's communicate!* rap.**

Computers and the internet

CD3 27

A **computer** is a complex machine that stores, **retrieves** and **processes** information. Today it's difficult to imagine a world without computers. We use computers to search for and send information, to do our homework, to play games, and we can even use computers to do our shopping!

The **internet** is a global network of computers. Every computer that is connected to the internet is part of that network, even your computer at home!

We use a **search engine** to look for information on the internet.

A **browser** is a program on your computer that allows us to visit a website.

A **website** is a place on the internet that gives us the information.

search engine

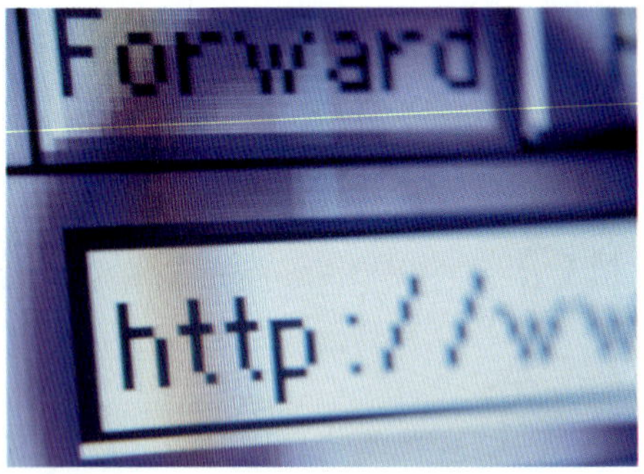

browser

website

store *(verb)* to save information on a computer.

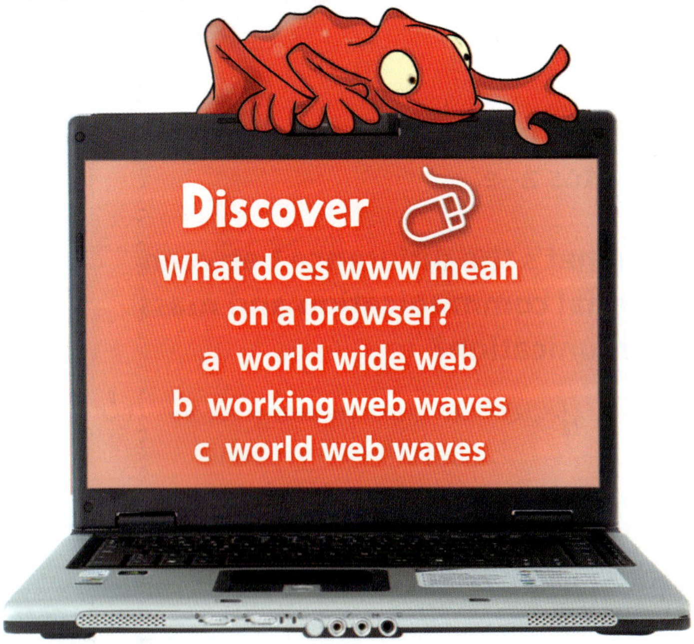

1 **What type of machine is a computer?**

2 **Copy and complete the sentence.**

A computer ______, retrieves and ______ information.

3 Me **What do you use computers for?**

Advertisements

CD3 28

All forms of mass communication have **advertisements**. Advertisements give information about products we can buy. They make toys look fun, they make clothes look beautiful and they make food look delicious.

But think before you buy something. Do you really need it? Be a **responsible** consumer.

1 Look at the advertisements a–c. Do you believe what they say? Do you want to buy any of these products? Why?

2 Do you sometimes buy things you don't need?

3 What is a responsible consumer?

consumer *(noun)*
a person who buys something.

Let's investigate! Advertisements

Investigate advertisements and record your results.

You need:

- some magazines

a Find advertisements in the magazines.
b Copy and complete the chart.

Product	Is it for adults, children or both?	How does it get your attention?	Do you want to buy the product?

The Science Club blog

CD3 29

CD3 30

A **blog** is a website where you can add new information all the time. There are millions of blogs about lots of different things, and they all look different, too. A blog gives you a voice on the internet. It's a place where you can share the things that you find interesting.

MY TRANSPORT FOR THE FUTURE

1 **Invent a form of transport for the future.**

- **a** Is it a form of public or private transport?
- **b** Is it for people or for goods?
- **c** Does it travel on land, on water or in the air?
- **d** Does it cause noise pollution or air pollution?

2 **Draw a picture of your vehicle.**

3 **Write a text to describe it.**

This is my transport for the future. It's a waterbus. It's a form of public transport. It can travel on land and on water, and it has eight wheels. It's very fast and it can travel long distances, but it doesn't cause noise pollution or air pollution.

REMEMBER!

on land
on water
in the air

Learning to learn

1 **Copy and complete the word maps.**

ferry train radio telephone motorbike plane van internet

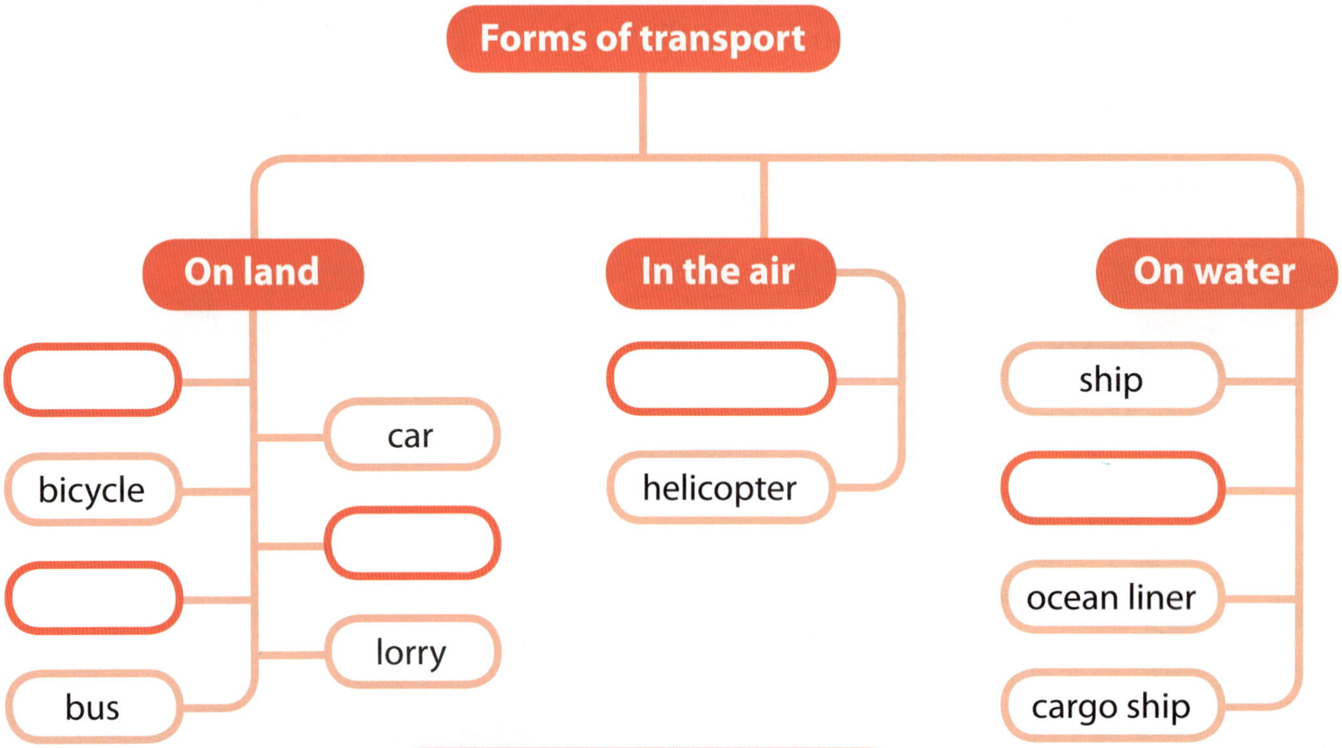

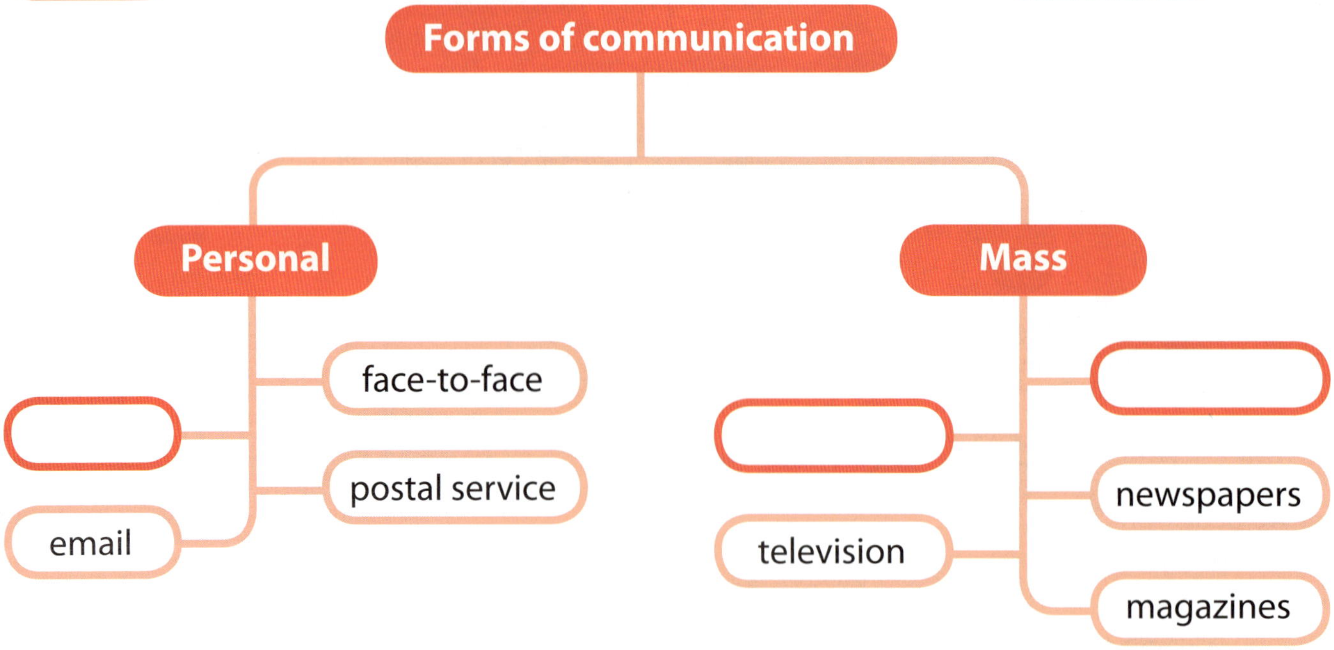

2 **Use the word maps to copy and complete the sentences.**

a Forms of transport can travel on ______ , in the air or on ______ .

b Forms of communication can be ______ communication or mass communication.

3 True or false? Copy the sentences and correct the ones that are false.

a Ferries and cargo ships travel on land.
b Planes and lorries are forms of air travel.
c Metro trains usually travel underground.
d Buses are a form of private transport.
e Motorbikes are a form of private transport.

4 Which is the odd one out? Why?

a **postal service / email / radio / telephone**
b **newspapers / telephone / television / internet**

. . . is the odd one out because . . .

5 Order and copy the letters to find out what a computer does with information.

troess | vieretrse | sspesroce

6 Order and copy the sentences about how television news is made.

An editor checks and prepares information for the newsreader.

Television cameras film the news.

Our televisions receive this information and we can watch the news.

A transmitter sends signals to our televisions.

Journalists and cameramen record and film important events and send information to editors.

The newsreader reads the news in the studio.

I can identify and classify different forms of transport.	☆ ☆ ☆
I know about different forms of personal communication.	☆ ☆ ☆
I know about different forms of mass communication.	☆ ☆ ☆
I am a responsible consumer.	☆ ☆ ☆

11 Work — The three job sectors

In this unit we're going to learn about the different jobs people do and how these people help us.

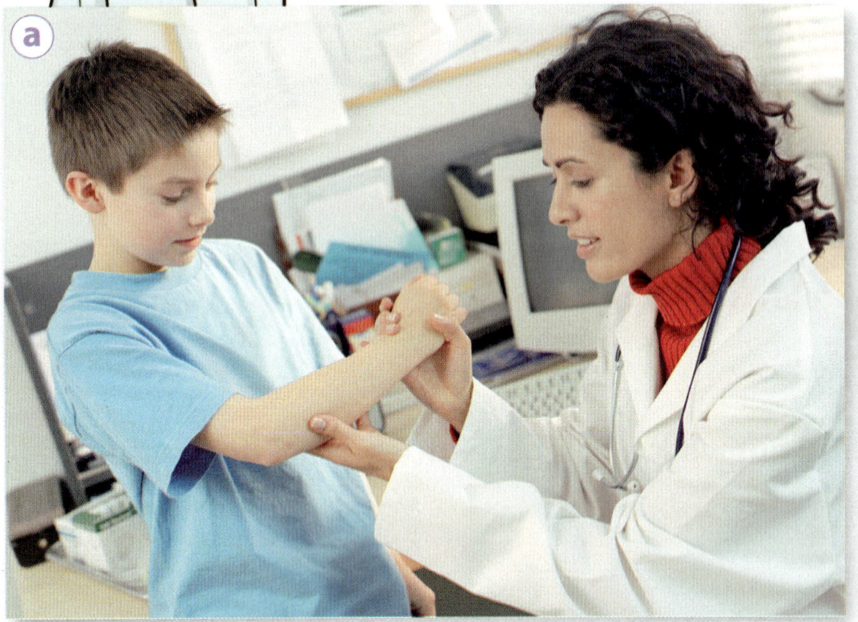

What do you want to be when you grow up? Do you want to do any of these jobs?

CD3 31

People have jobs to earn money. We call this money a **salary**. People use their salary to buy food, clothes, a car and even a house.

There are many different types of jobs and every job is important.

CD3 32

We can classify jobs into three sectors called the **primary**, **secondary** and **tertiary** sectors. People with jobs in the **primary sector** obtain or process natural products. People with jobs in the **secondary sector** transform natural products into manufactured products. People with jobs in the **tertiary sector** provide a service.

1 CD3 33 **Say the *Jobs* chant.**

2 Why do people have jobs?

3 Copy and complete the chart to classify the jobs.

Primary sector	Secondary sector	Tertiary sector

Let's investigate! Jobs where we live

In which job sector do you think most people in Spain work? Listen and read, then look at the pie chart to find out the answer. Both give the same information, but which is easier to understand?

CD3 34

In Spain, about 5% of people work in the primary sector, 30% in the secondary sector and 65% in the tertiary sector.

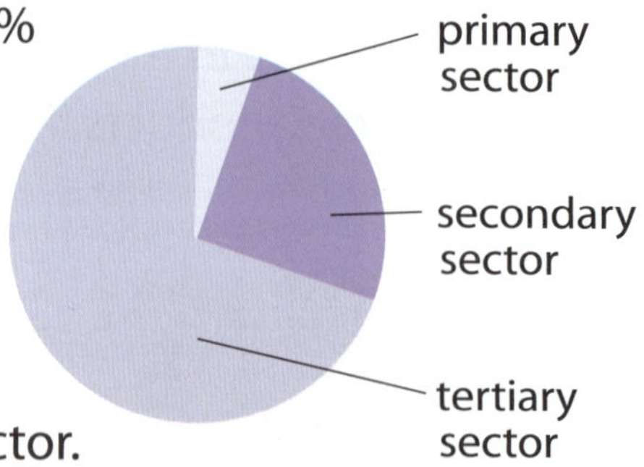

Investigate job sectors.

Which job sector do most of your classmates' families work in?

Do a survey of jobs.

a Ask your classmates what jobs people in their families do.

b Classify the jobs into the three sectors.

c Draw a graph to show the results.

Primary sector: Arable farming

CD3 35

The farming of **crops** is called **arable farming**. People have been growing crops for thousands of years. Today, science is important in farming because arable farmers need to know what kinds of crops will grow well in their soil and how to look after these crops. They also need to know how to sell these crops. Farms are very important because they give us nearly all the food we eat.

wheat

bread

olive tree

olive oil

corn

cereals

rice

paella

CD3 36

All crops need water to grow, but some crops need just rainwater. We call these crops **dry crops**. You already know that an olive tree can grow in poor soil. Olive trees, wheat and grapes are some examples of dry crops.

dry crops

Tomatoes, potatoes and rice are some crops that need more water than just rainwater to grow well. These are called **irrigated crops**. Farmers use irrigation to give these crops the extra water they need.

irrigated crops

1 **Why is science important in farming?**

2 **Look at the pictures above and write sentences.**

We use wheat to make bread.

3 **What other foods are made from the crops in the pictures?**

4 **What's the difference between dry crops and irrigated crops?**

Primary sector: Livestock farming

Livestock farming consists of buying and selling farm animals such as cows, pigs, sheep and chickens. Farmers rear farm animals for products, such as their meat, milk or skins. There are different types of livestock farming, including **cattle farming**, **pig farming**, **sheep farming** and **poultry farming**.

a

b

c

d

There are two types of livestock farming: **intensive farming** and **free-range farming**. Intensive farming means that the farmer rears the animals and feeds them in small spaces. In free-range farming the animals live outside, and they have more space to move and to eat grass.

rear *(verb)* to look after farm animals.

How milk is produced

1

The farmer feeds the cows.

2
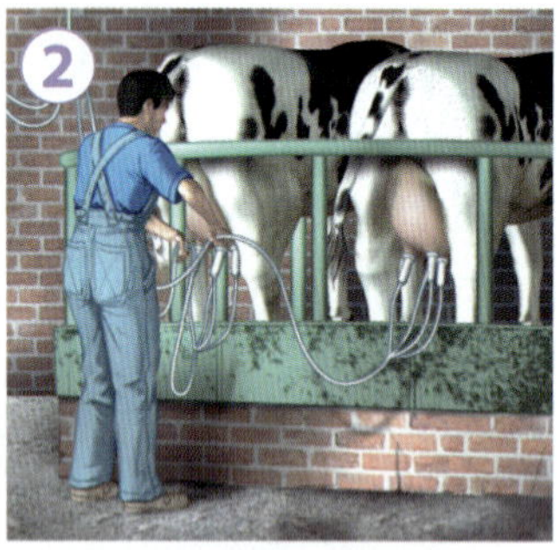
The farmer milks the cows.

3

The milk is processed in factories.

4
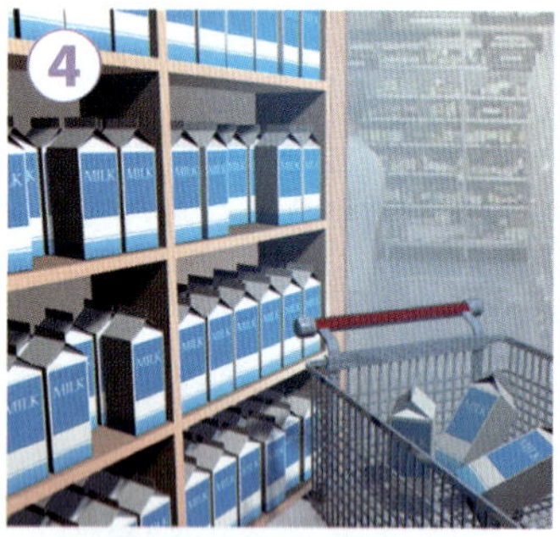
We buy the milk from the shops.

1 **Can you remember the different products we get from farm animals?**

2 **Look at photos a–d and identify the types of livestock farming.**

3 **Which photos show free-range farming?**

4 **Which do you think is better, intensive farming or free-range farming? Why?**

5 **Listen and learn about how milk is produced. Find out and describe how another animal product is produced.**

Natural resources from the sea

CD3 39

Fishing involves catching fish and shellfish from rivers, lakes and seas. There are two types of sea fishing: **coastal fishing** and **deep-sea fishing**.

Coastal fishing happens near the coast. The fishermen go out to sea every day in small boats. They return to sell the fresh fish in fish markets. **Deep-sea fishing** happens a long way from the coast. The fishermen go out to sea for weeks or months in bigger boats. They freeze and store the fish on the boats so they can sell them when they return.

shellfish *(noun)* sea creatures with an exoskeleton, e.g. crabs and mussels.

Natural resources from the Earth

CD3 40

Mining involves taking natural resources from the Earth.

A miner mines rocks and minerals, such as **coal**, **stone**, **salt** and even **gold**. Miners have to work in deep tunnels underground. This work is hard and can be dangerous.

DID YOU KNOW?

The largest gold nugget was discovered in a mine in Australia. It weighed over 70 kilos – that's as heavy as a human adult!

1 **What are the differences between coastal fishing and deep-sea fishing?**

2 **Does tinned fish come from coastal fishing or deep-sea fishing?**

3 **What natural resources do miners take from the Earth?**

4 **Look at the photo of the miner. Why do you think mining is hard work?**

Secondary sector: Craft and industry

CD3 41

Manufactured products are made by transforming natural products into other materials. This can be done by **craft** or by **industry**.

Craft workers use their hands or simple tools to make manufactured products and **industrial workers** use machines to make these products.

Products made by craft workers are **unique**. This means that each object is different.

a craft worker

Products made by industrial workers are **mass-produced**. This means that lots of products are made very quickly and they are all the same. Mass-produced products are usually made in **factories**, where lots of people work together with machines to make the product.

CD3 42

How toys are made in a factory

1 Machines make the parts of the toys.

2 Machines paint the toys.

3 Factory workers build the toys.

4 Factory workers package the toys.

1 **What are the differences between products made by craft workers and products made by industrial workers?**

2 Me **Can you identify manufactured products in your classroom? Do you think these are made by craft workers or by industrial workers? Why?**

3 CD3 42 **Listen and learn about how toys are made in a factory.**

4 **Which toy do you think is more expensive: the one made by the craft worker or the one made in a factory? Why?**

CD3 43

Many people have jobs that provide a service. We can classify these jobs into different groups, for example: **education**, **health care**, **tourism**, **transport**, **retail** and **administration**.

People with jobs in **education** help us learn new things. People with jobs in **health care** look after our health and the health of animals, too. People with jobs in **tourism** help us when we go on holiday. People with jobs in **transport** take us from one place to another or transport goods. People with jobs in **retail** help sell products to customers. People with jobs in **administration** help organise work in offices.

1 **Look at photos a–f and identify the jobs.**

2 **In which service industry groups do the people in the photos work?**

3 **Can you think of any more jobs that provide a service?**

4 Me **How do people in the service industry help you every day?**

5 CD3 44 **Sing the *Work* song.**

The Science Club volunteers

To be a **volunteer** means to give your time and energy to work that you're interested in.

Volunteers don't get a salary, but they can make a difference and even make new friends, too!

Could you be a volunteer?

MY SCIENCE PROJECT

A JOB DESCRIPTION

1 Interview an adult about the work they do.

a What's their job?

b Which job sector do they work in?

c Describe what they do.

2 Write a text.

3 Take a photo, find a photo from a magazine or draw a picture to illustrate your text.

REMEMBER!

He / She works ...
He / She helps ...

Roberto García is a firefighter. He works in the tertiary sector. Roberto helps put out fires and saves people's lives. His job is sometimes very hard and it can be dangerous.

Learning to learn

1 Copy and complete the word map.

health care   industrial workers   administration
fishing   transport   arable farming

Work

The primary sector

- ______
- livestock farming
- ______
- mining

The secondary sector

- craft workers
- ______

The tertiary sector

- ______
- education
- ______
- tourism
- retail
- ______

2 Match and write the sentences.

a People who work in the primary sector	provide a service.
b People who work in the secondary sector	obtain or process natural products.
c People who work in the tertiary sector	transform natural products into manufactured products.

3 Copy and complete the sentences about the types of crops in arable farming.

______ need just rainwater to grow.

______ need more water than just rainwater to grow well.

4 Copy and complete the chart with the sentences.

Use machines to make manufactured products.

Use their hands or simple tools to make manufactured products.

Products are mass-produced.

Products are unique.

Craft workers	Industrial workers

5 Copy and complete the sentence to classify jobs that provide a service.

health care   transport   retail   tourism   education   administration

We can classify jobs in the service industry into different groups. For example:

______ ,

______ ,

______ ,

______ ,

______ and

______ .

I can identify jobs in the primary, secondary and tertiary sectors. ☆ ☆ ☆

I know about arable farming and livestock farming. ☆ ☆ ☆

I know some differences between craft workers and industrial workers. ☆ ☆ ☆

I can identify and classify jobs that provide a service. ☆ ☆ ☆

12 Where we live

Places

In this unit we're going to learn about the places where people live. We're also going to learn how to make and use maps. Look at the photos. Where does Nico live? Where does Clara live?

CD3 47

Most people live together in small places like **villages**, big places like **towns** or very big places like **cities**.

Villages are small places with **few inhabitants**, which means that not many people live there. There are **few services** in villages, but there is usually a square, a church and a town hall. There is often a main street with shops, too. Many people who live in villages work in arable or livestock farming or in tourism.

Towns and cities are large places with **many inhabitants**. There are squares, parks and churches in towns and cities, and there is a town hall, too. There are many shops and there are also **many services**. People who live in towns and cities work in a variety of jobs. They can work in offices, banks, hospitals and factories.

DID YOU KNOW?

The highest village in Spain is Trevélez in the province of Granada. It's in the mountains at 1476 metres above sea level.

1 **Look at the photos. What differences can you see?**

2 CD3 48 **Listen to Clara and Nico talking about where they live.**

3 **Choose the correct words and write the sentences.**

a Villages have **few** / **many** inhabitants.
b Towns and cities have **few** / **many** inhabitants.
c There are **few** / **many** services in villages.
d There are **few** / **many** services in towns and cities.

4 **What types of jobs do many inhabitants of villages have? What sectors do these people work in?**

5 Me **Where would you prefer to live; in a village or a town or city? Why?**

Places change

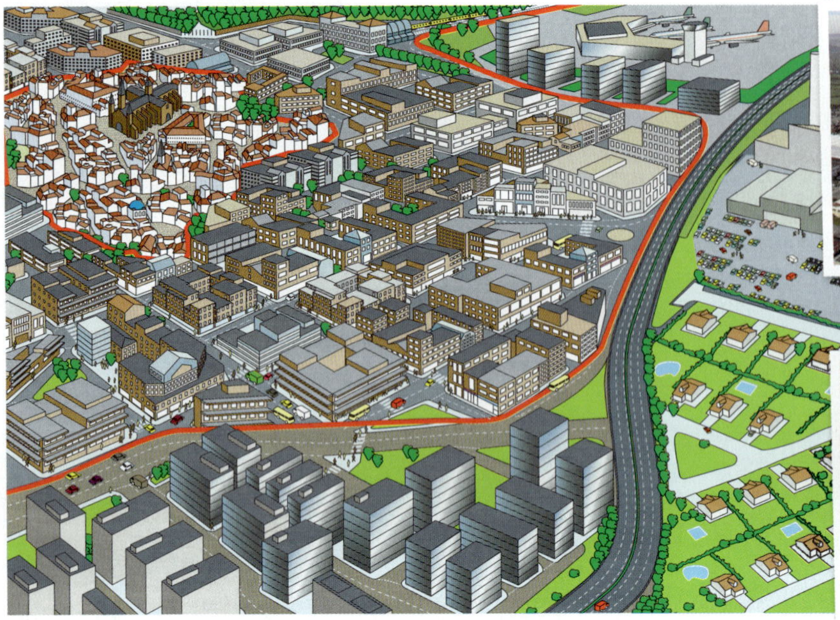

CD3 50

There are different parts to a city.

The **historic centre** is the oldest part of a city. The streets are usually narrow and the buildings are old. The main square, town hall and churches are usually found in this part of a city.

When the number of inhabitants in a city grows, new neighbourhoods are built. This **new part** of a city has wide, straight streets and the buildings are new. There are usually lots of flats, offices and shops in this new part of a city.

On the **outskirts** of a city, there is usually lots of space to build new buildings, such as more flats, offices and shops. We can find factories and sometimes airports on the outskirts.

CD3 51

Villages can also change. Some villages get bigger and turn into towns. Other villages are abandoned when the inhabitants go to live and work in towns and cities.

1 **Look at the picture and identify the historic centre, the new part and the outskirts of the city.**

2 **What differences can you see between these parts of the city?**

3 **In which part of the city do you think you can find these buildings?**

a factory **b** main square **c** airport
d flats **e** town hall **f** hospital

4 **Look at Clara's photos of a city. In which parts of the city do you think Clara took these photos?**

5 CD3 52 **Sing the *City* song.**

6 **What can happen to villages over time?**

Services in a city

There are many different types of **services** in a city. There are education services, such as **schools**, health services, such as **hospitals**, cultural services, such as **libraries**; and things that help us, such as **zebra crossings** and **telephone boxes**. All of these are **visible services**, but there are also many types of services we can't see that are under our feet!

These **underground services** are also important. **Water pipes**, **gas pipes**, **electricity cables**, **telephone cables**, **sewer pipes** and **metro trains** are all examples of underground services.

Services in a city are for everyone to use, so it's important that we respect them!

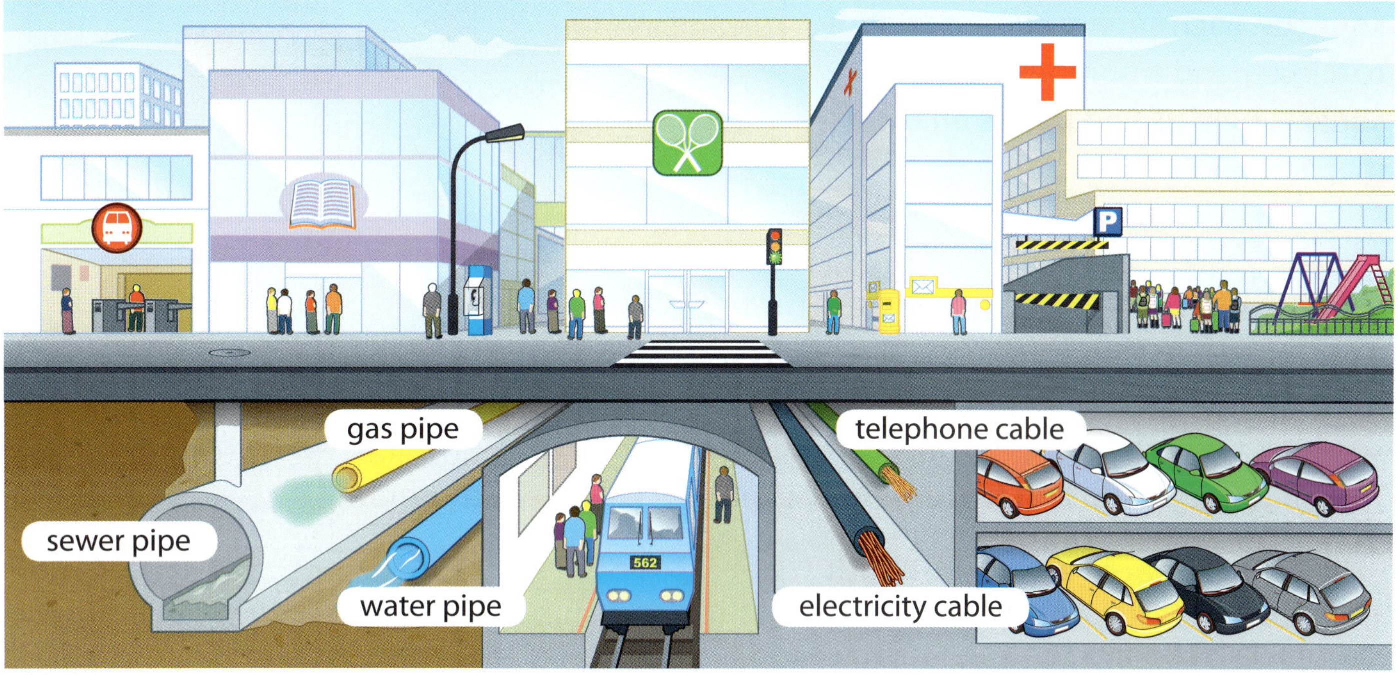

1 **Say the *Visible services* chant.**

2 **Say the *Underground services* chant.**

3 **Look at the picture. What visible services can you identify?**

4 **Which visible services do you think are the most important? Why?**

5 **Which underground services do you think are the most important? Why?**

6 **What visible services are there in your neighbourhood?**

7 **Why is it important to respect the services in a city?**

Maps

CD3 56

Maps show us where things are and they make places easier to find. City maps show us streets and have symbols for important buildings and places in the city. We can find out what these symbols mean by looking at the **key** on the map.

City maps are usually divided into **squares**. Each square corresponds to a letter and a number. These squares help us find places on the map easily.

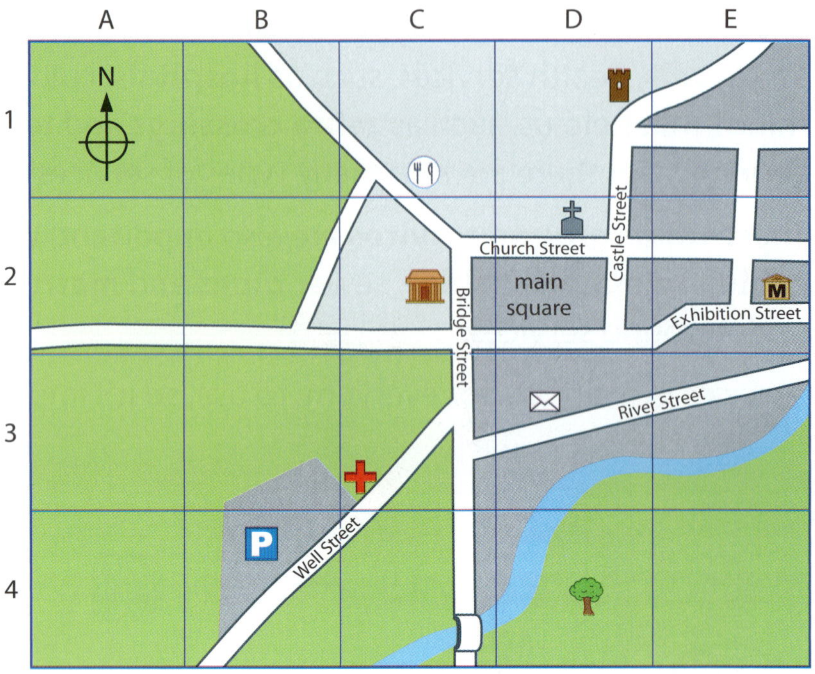

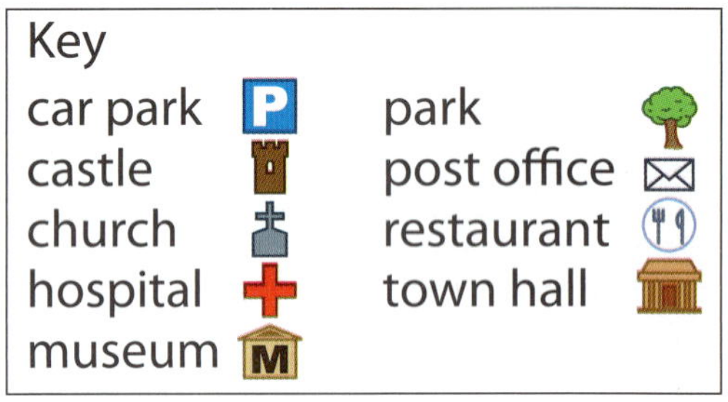

symbol *(noun)* a picture or shape used to represent something.

1 **Identify a natural feature on the map.**

2 **Which places are in the north / east / south / west of the city?**

3 **Which places are in these squares?**

a D1 b D3 c C1

4 **In which squares can you find these places?**

a the hospital b the museum
c the church

5 **Design a symbol for the following places:**

a school b tourist information office
c sports centre d airport e factory

6 **Choose a square on the map to put these places and say why.**

Make a map of an area in your school.

How can you help people find places in your school?

Divide a piece of paper into squares and give each square a letter and a number.

Map an area in your school. Include a key and design symbols for the important places.

Give your map to a friend. Can they use it to find places?

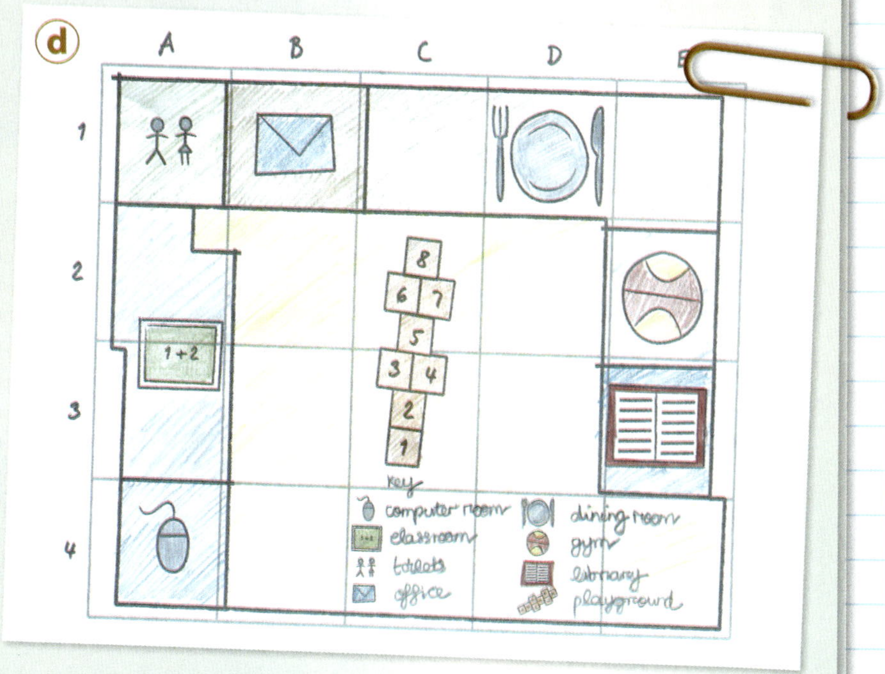

Lost!

CD3 57

CD3 58

Villages, towns and cities change all the time. This means that new places sometimes aren't on older maps.

Today, many people have a **GPS** in their cars. These machines communicate with satellites which orbit Earth to fix their location. A computer in the GPS then plans the route to the destination.

My Science Presentation

WHERE I LIVE

1 Find out information about the village, town or city where you live.

- a What kinds of services are there?
- b What forms of transport can you use?
- c Which job sector do you think most inhabitants work in?
- d What kinds of jobs do these people have?

2 Write a text using your information.

3 Find photos or postcards of where you live or draw pictures.

4 Use your text and your pictures to make a poster.

5 Present your poster to the class.

Learning to learn

1 Copy and complete the word map.

few services | low buildings | villages | wide streets | many inhabitants

Where we live

- ____
  - few inhabitants
  - narrow streets
  - ____
  - ____
- towns and cities
  - ____
  - ____
  - many services
  - high buildings

2 Use the word map to copy and complete the sentences.

a Villages are small places with ____ inhabitants. Villages have short, ____ streets. There are ____ services. Buildings in villages are ____.

b Towns and cities are large places with ____ inhabitants. Towns and cities have long, ____ streets. There are ____ services. Buildings in towns and cities can be ____.

3 Copy and match the definitions.

a The oldest part of the city.

b When the number of inhabitants in the historic centre grows, new neighbourhoods are built here.

c There is usually lots of space to build new buildings here.

outskirts | historic centre | new part

4 Copy the chart and classify the visible and underground services.

telephone cable | traffic light | electricity cable | sewer pipe | post box | zebra crossing | water pipe | street lamp | telephone box | gas pipe

Visible services	Underground services

5 Identify these places on the map. Which squares can you find them in?

a 

b 

c 

d 

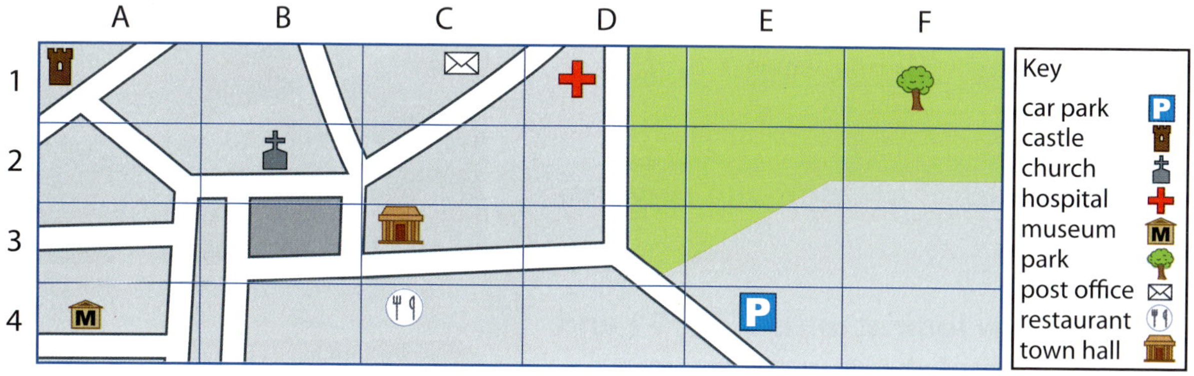

I know the differences between villages, towns and cities. ☆ ☆ ☆

I know how places can change. ☆ ☆ ☆

I can identify visible services and underground services in a city. ☆ ☆ ☆

I can use a city map. ☆ ☆ ☆

Units 9–12 review

Listen to the quiz and write the answers to the questions.

CD3 59

SCIENCE CLUB QUIZ

1 What is soil made up of?

2 What do we call the bottom layer of soil?

3 Name two vehicles that can transport goods.

4 Name two forms of sea transport.

5 What are five forms of mass communication?

6 What do we call the money people earn from their jobs?

7 What are the two types of sea fishing called?

8 What is the oldest part of a city called?

9 What three things can we use to find our way around villages, towns and cities?

10 Name two types of underground services.

Now look at units 9, 10, 11 and 12 and check your answers.

CD3 60 **Listen and check your answers.**

How did you do?

8–10 points	5–7 points	0–4 points
Excellent	Good	Try again

SCIENCE CHALLENGE

Find a friend. Decide who is Pupil A and who is Pupil B. Take it in turns to ask and answer the questions in the Science Challenge.

PUPIL A

1. *This is the most productive layer of the soil.*
2. *Only hardy plants like olive trees can grow in this type of soil.*
3. *Many plants can grow well in this type of soil.*
4. *This is an old form of communication.*
5. *What can newspapers and magazines also be called?*
6. *People with jobs in this sector transform natural products into manufactured products.*
7. *People with jobs in this sector provide a service.*
8. *Products made by this type of worker are unique.*
9. *These are large places with many inhabitants and many services.*
10. *This part of a city usually has lots of space to build new buildings. In this area there are usually more flats, offices, shops and factories.*

PUPIL B

1. *This is the middle layer of the soil. There is very little humus.*
2. *Only very hardy plants like cacti can grow in this type of soil.*
3. *This is the fastest form of transport.*
4. *We must be connected to the internet to use this form of personal communication.*
5. *This is a place on the internet that gives you information.*
6. *People with jobs in this sector obtain or process natural products.*
7. *Products made by this type of worker are mass-produced.*
8. *These are small places with few inhabitants and few services.*
9. *This part of a city has large, wide streets and the buildings are new.*
10. *This is an underground service that takes gas to our homes so we can cook and keep our homes warm in winter.*

Can you remember the definitions of these words?

hardy *(adj)* ...
rare *(adj)* ...
store *(verb)* ...
consumer *(noun)* ...
rear *(verb)* ...
shellfish *(noun)* ...
symbol *(noun)* ...

Answers on Photocopiable Resources CD, Unit 12.

1 Living and non-living things

Nutrition

People need food.

Animals need food.

Plants need water.

Interaction

People interact.

Penguins interact to keep warm.

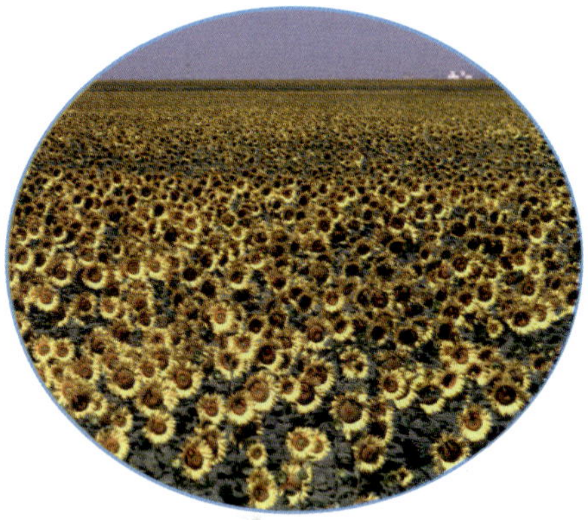

Sunflowers interact with the Sun.

Reproduction

People have babies.

Some animals lay eggs.

Plants produce seeds for new plants to grow.

Our eyes are the organs of sight.

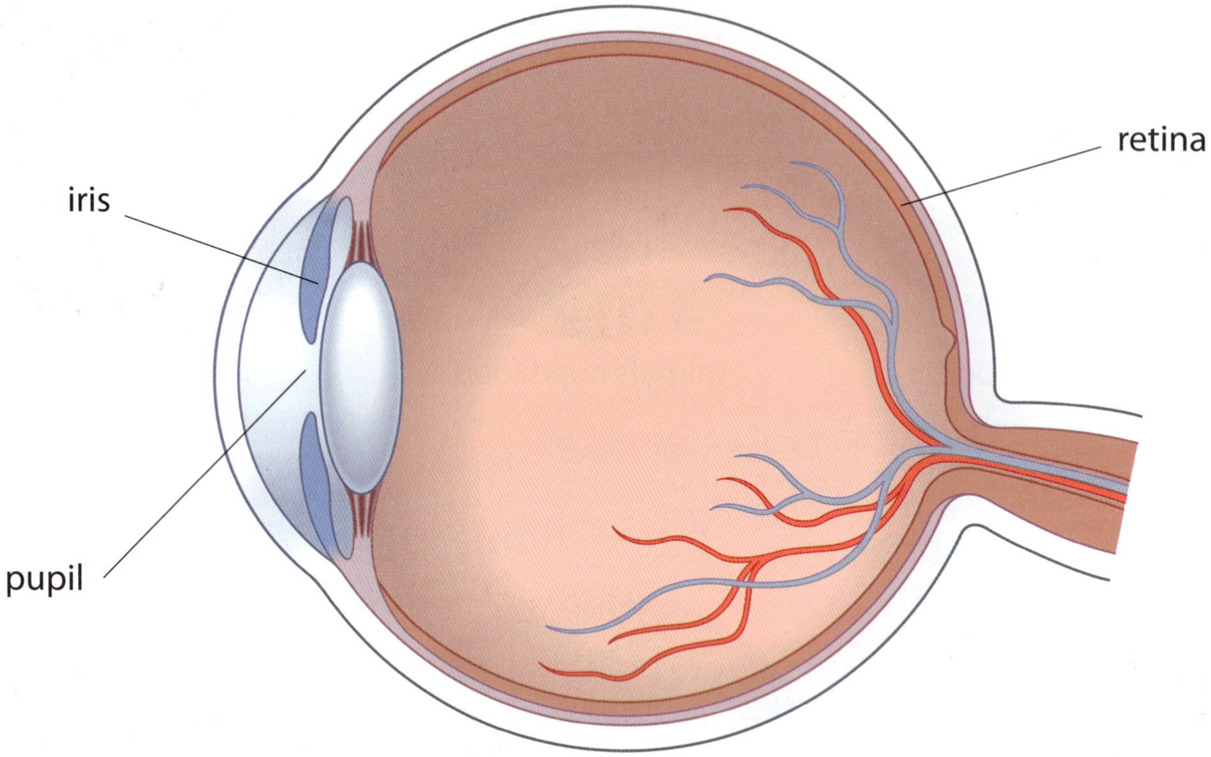

Our ears are the organs of hearing.

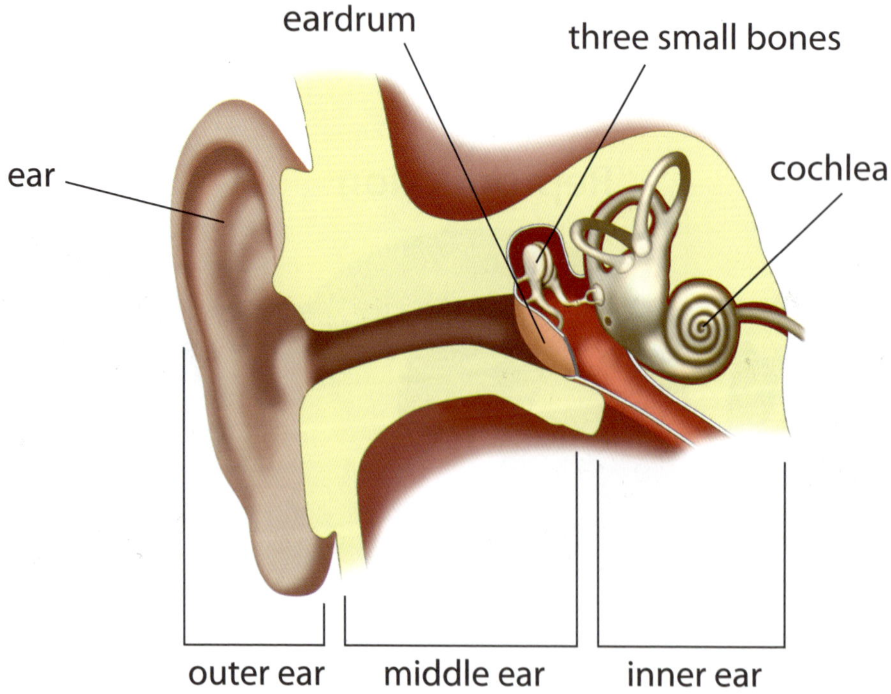

Our skin is the organ of touch.

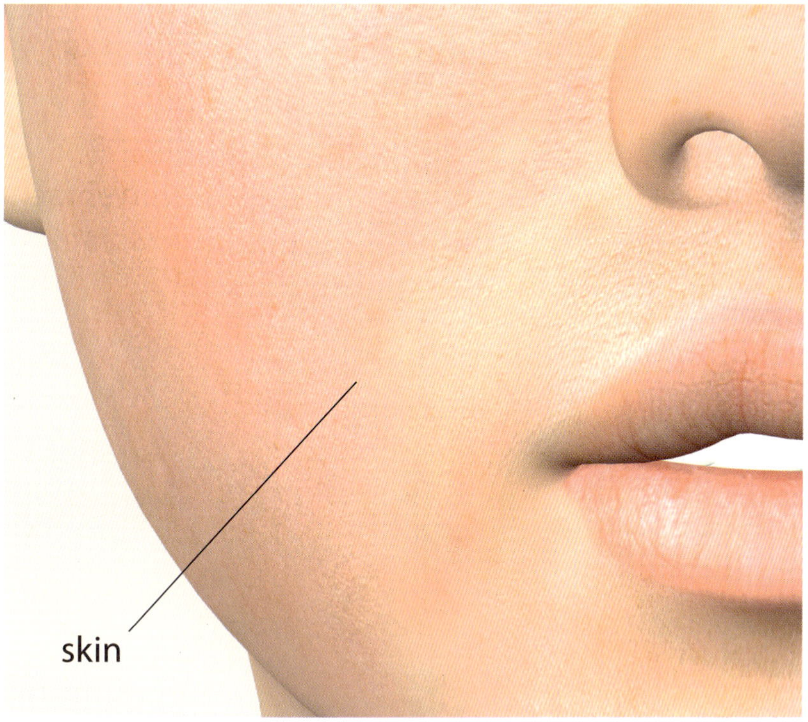

Our tongue is the organ of taste.

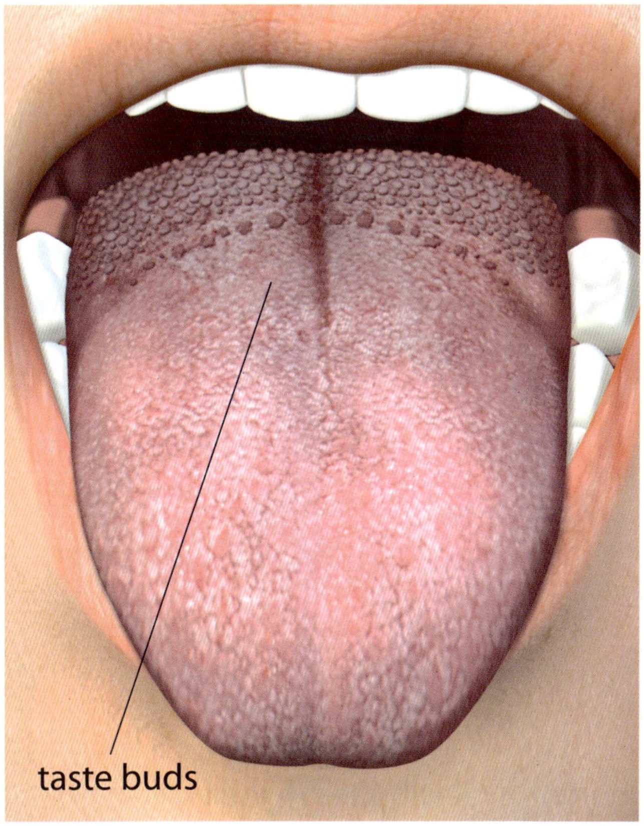

Our nose is the organ of smell.

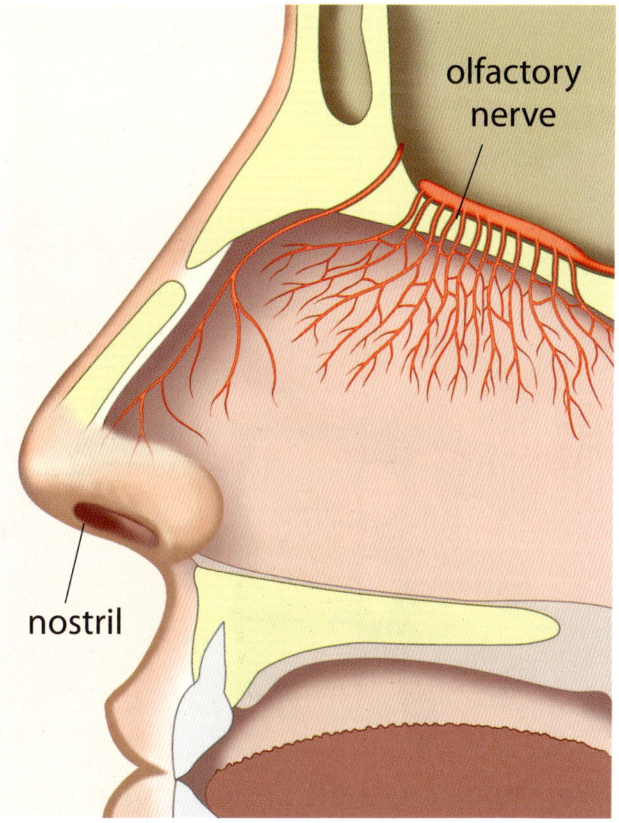

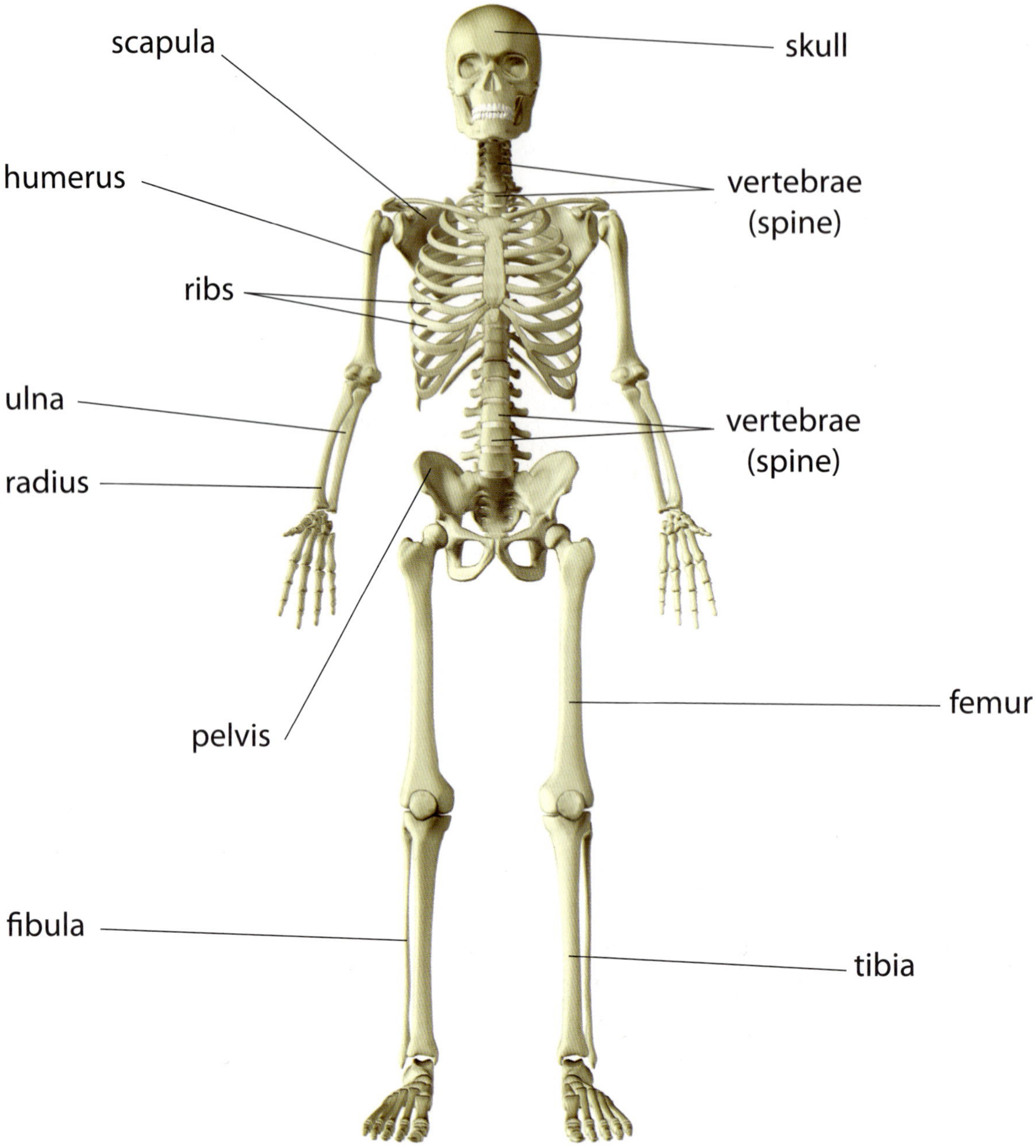

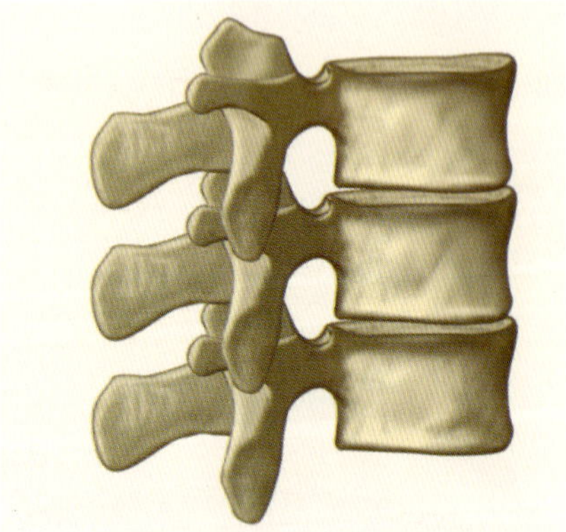

Vertebrae are short bones.

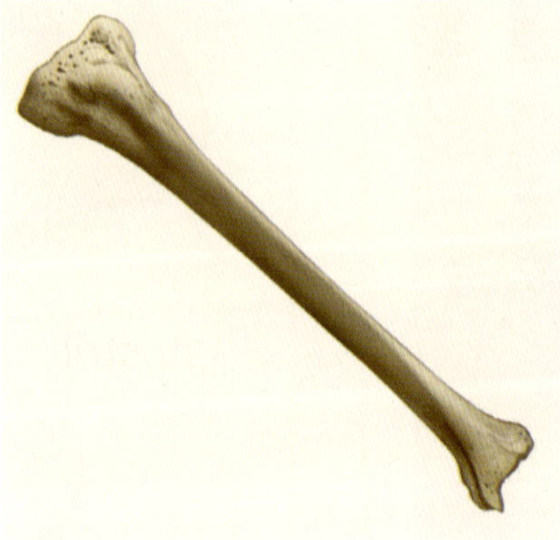

The tibia is a long bone.

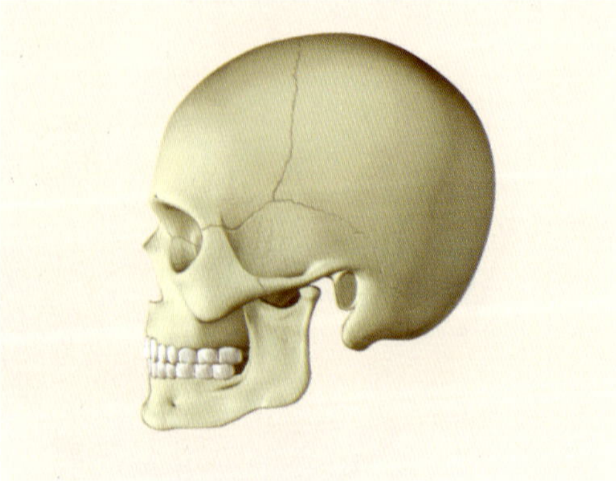

The bones in the skull are flat.

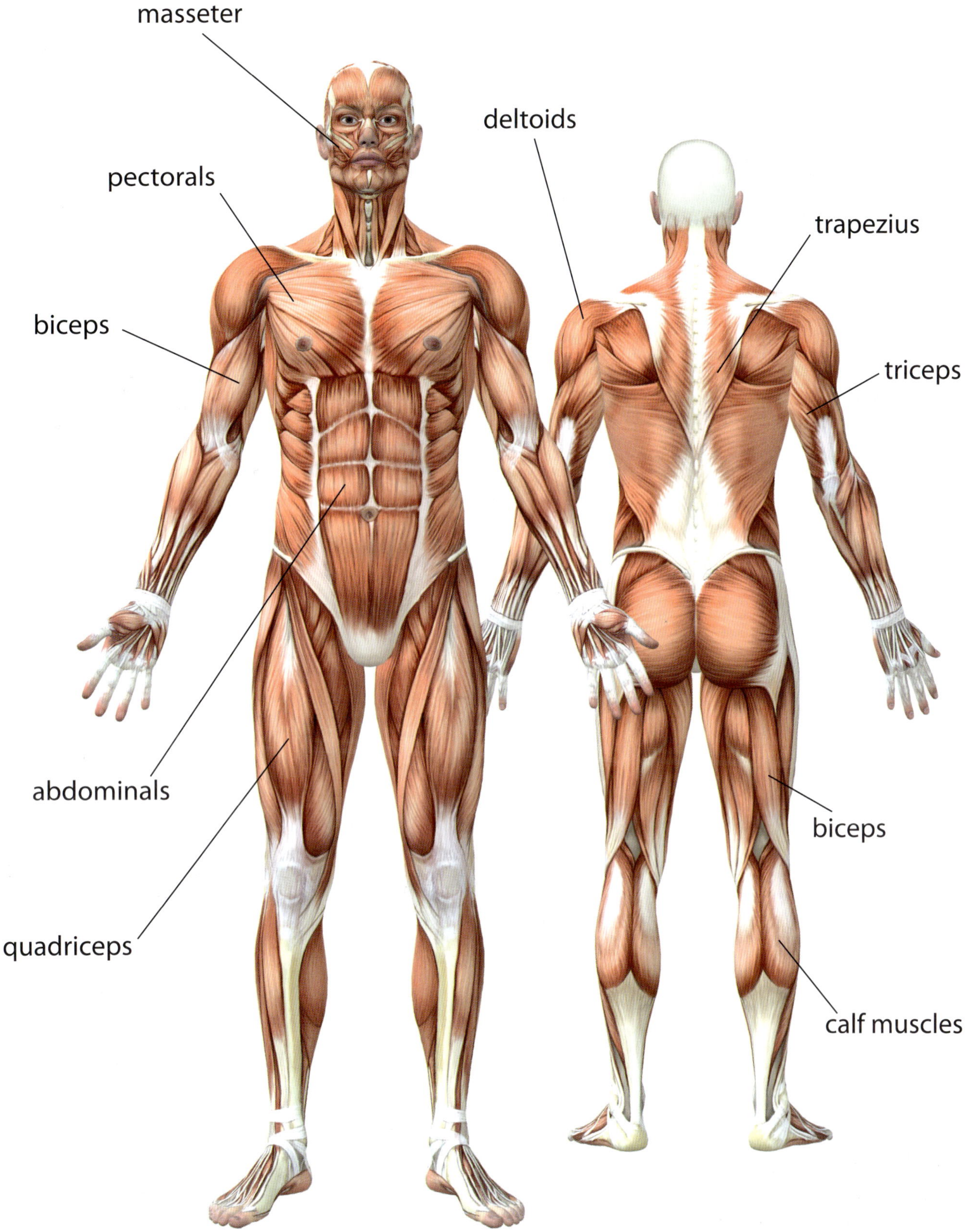
masseter
deltoids
pectorals
trapezius
biceps
triceps
abdominals
biceps
quadriceps
calf muscles

Vertebrates

chameleon

duck

fish

lizard

toad

whale

Invertebrates

butterfly

crab

lobster

mussel

spider

worm

Viviparous

elephant and calf

horse and foal

lioness and cub

Oviparous

crocodile

frog

insect

lizard

penguin

Parts of plants

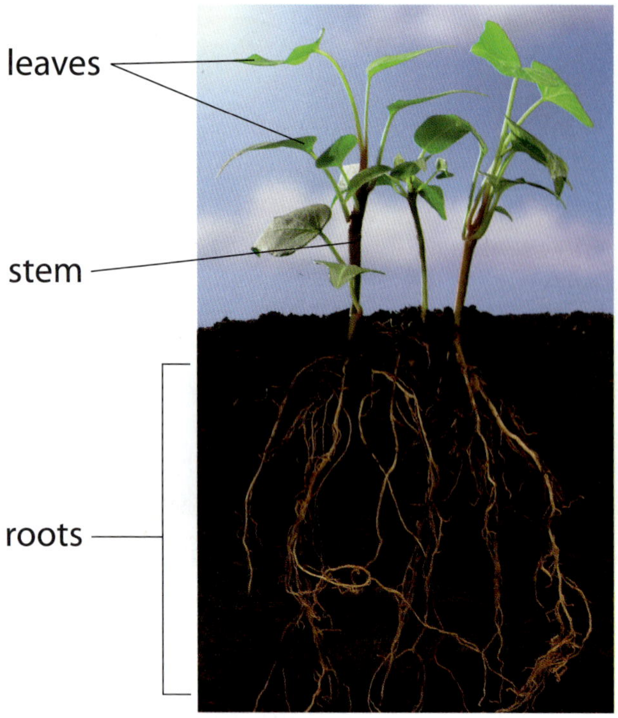

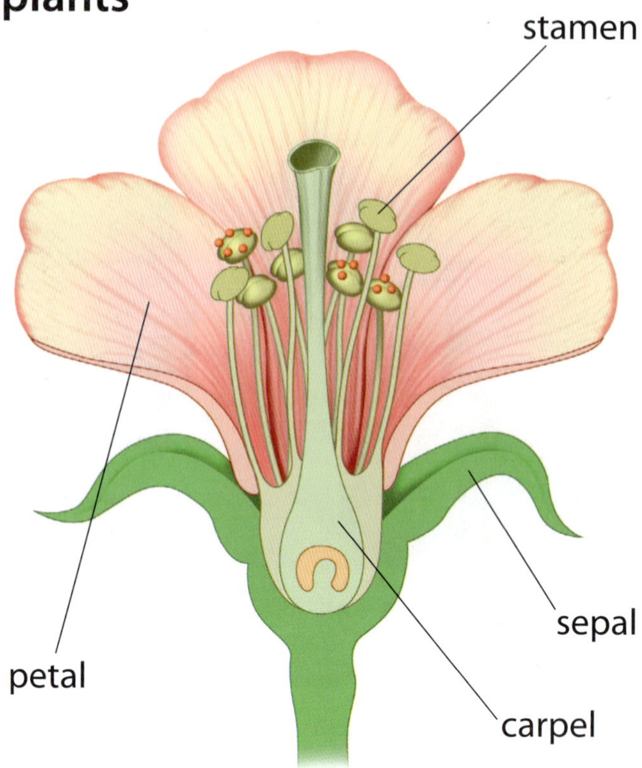

Leaf margins

dentate

entire

lobed

palmate

serrate

sinuate

Plants give us …

… seeds to make food.

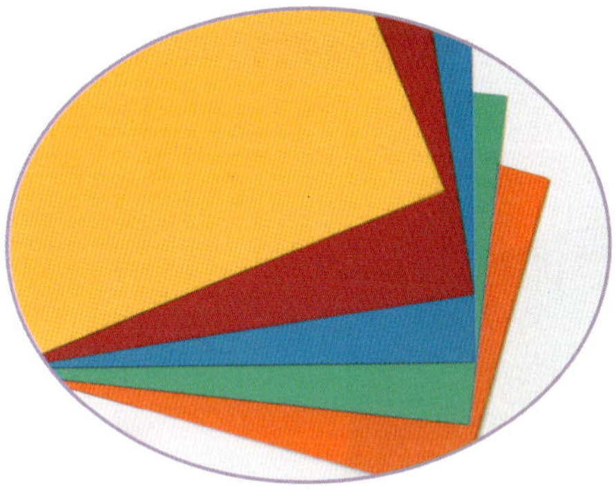

… paper to write on.

… wood to make furniture.

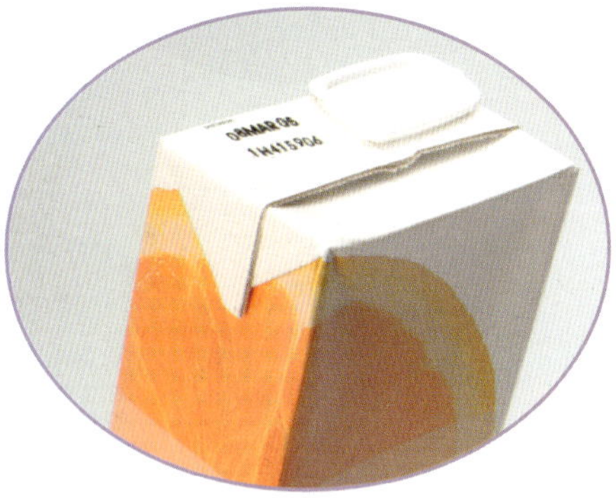

… vitamins and minerals to grow and stay healthy.

… wood to give us heat and shelter.

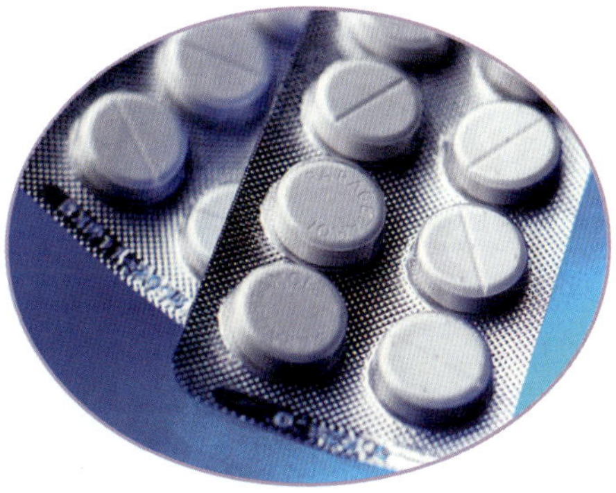

… medicines to make us well.

… cotton to make clothes.

… oxygen to breathe.

Picture dictionary

Habitats

Arctic region

desert

savannah

temperate forest

tropical rainforest

The food chain

producer

consumer

consumer

decomposer

habitat

A habitat is a specific place where living things live.

population

A population is a group of the same living things that live in the same place at the same time.

community

A community is formed when populations interact with each other.

ecosystem

An ecosystem is formed when communities interact with other communities and their surroundings.

clouds

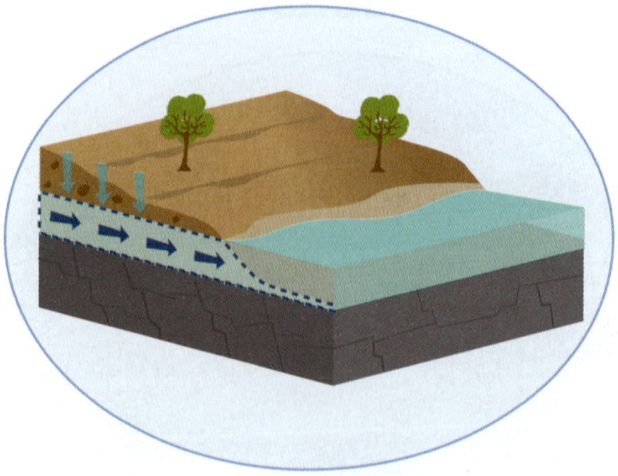

groundwater

icecaps

lake

reservoir

river

sea

Wind

calm

breeze

gale

hurricane

anemometer

weather vane

The water cycle

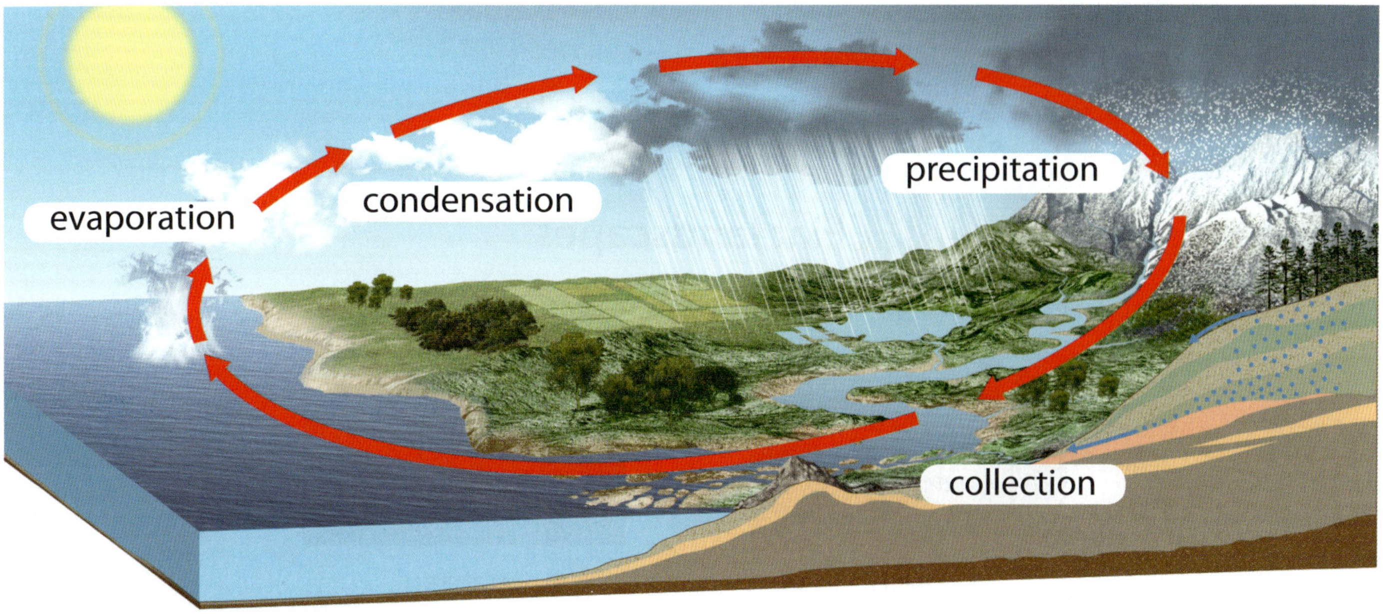

Mountain landscapes

hill

mountain

valley

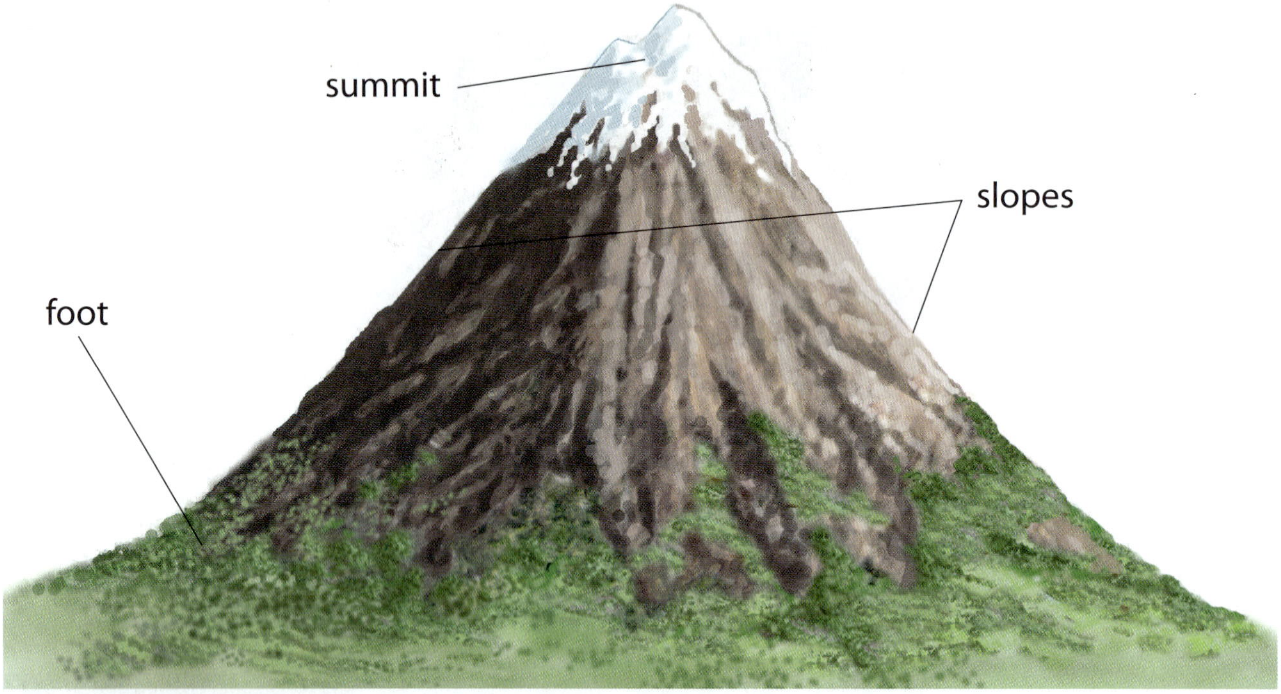

Flat landscapes

plain

plateau

Coastal landscapes

archipelago

bay

beach

cape

cliff

island

Rivers

meander

mouth

source

tributaries

Soil layers

Types of soil

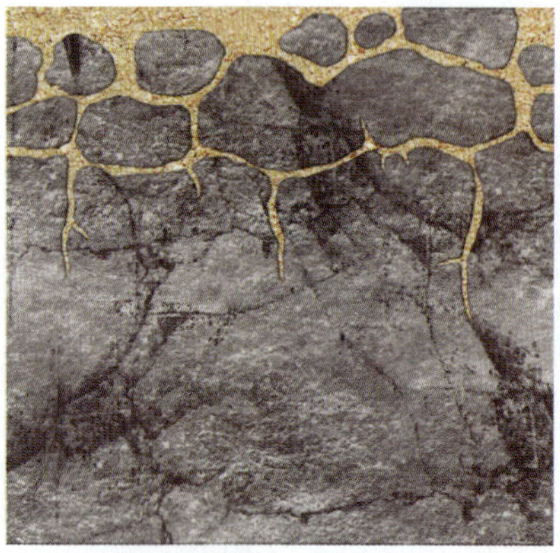

arid soil

fertile soil

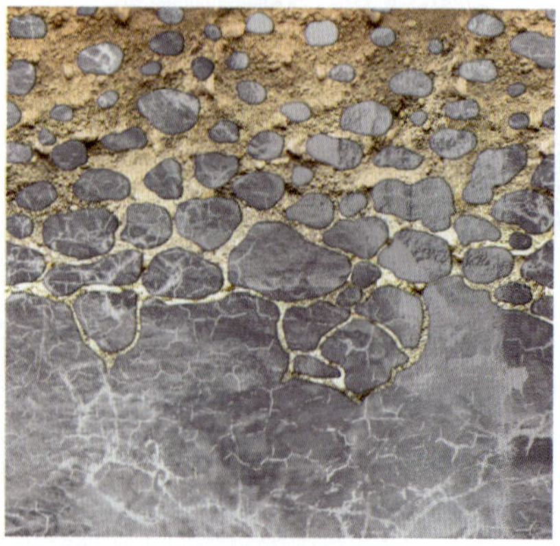

poor soil

The soil ecosystem

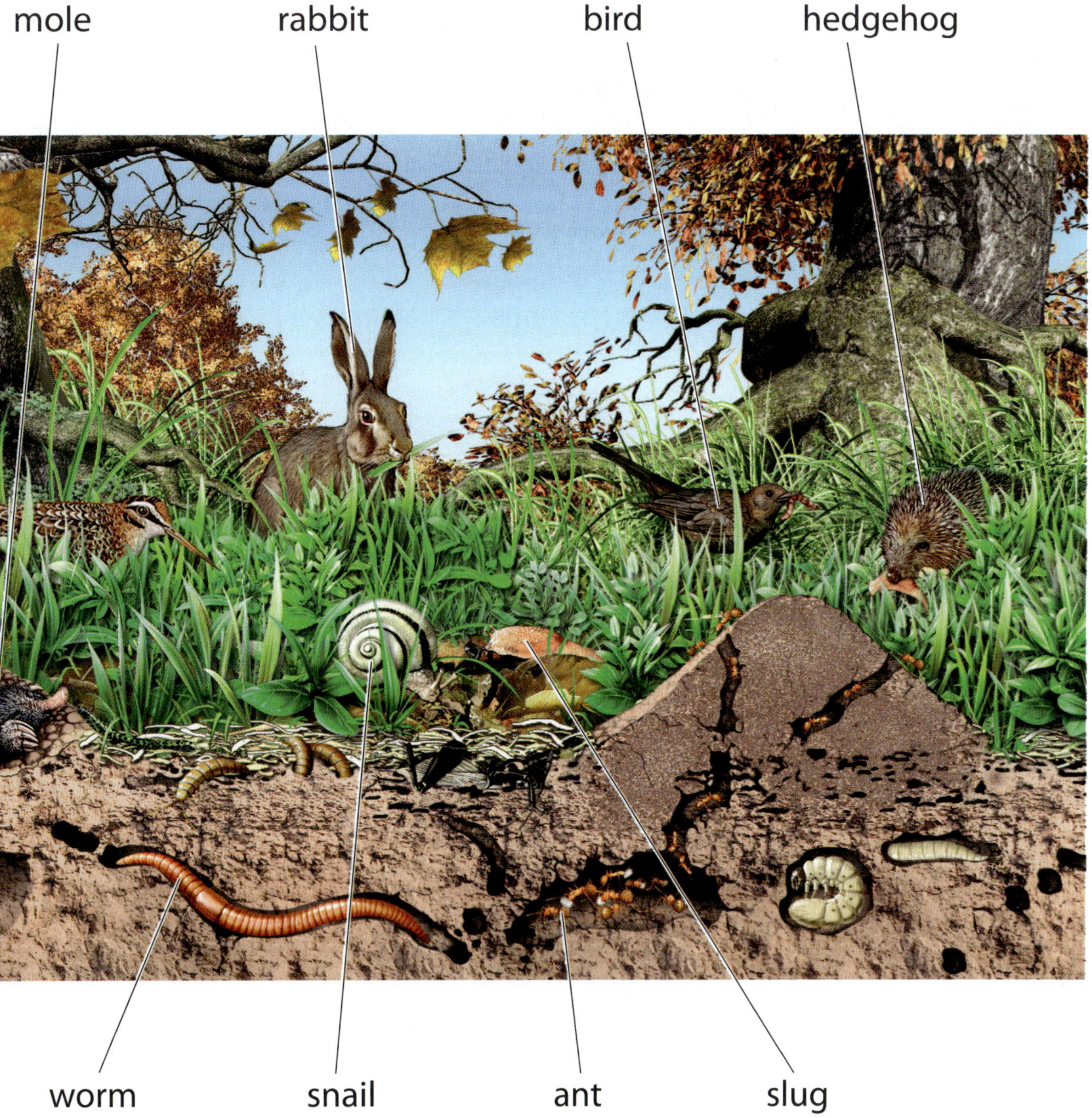

Land transport

bicycle

bus

car

lorry

metro train

motorbike

train

van

Air and sea transport

cargo ship

ferry

helicopter

plane

Personal communication

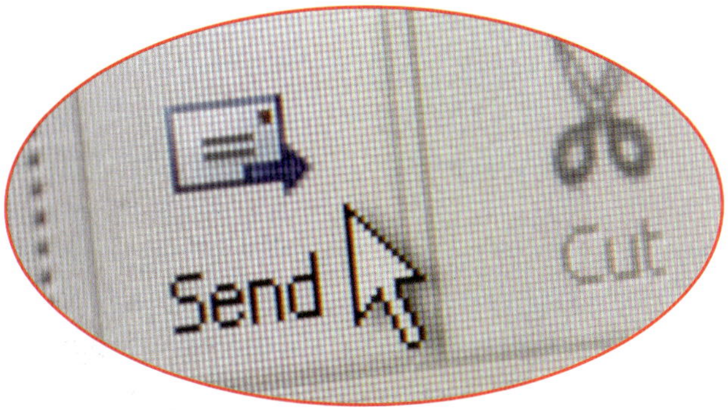

email

face-to-face

postal service

telephone

Mass communication

internet

magazines

newspapers

radio

television

The primary sector

farmer

fisherman

miner

The secondary sector

builder

craft worker

factory worker

The tertiary sector

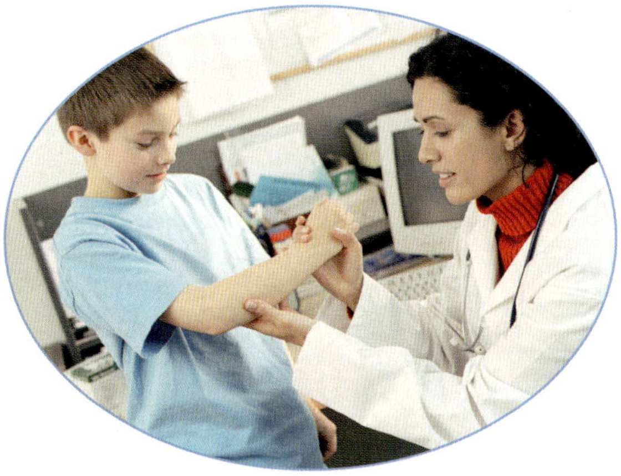

doctor

hairdresser

office worker

retail assistant

taxi driver

teacher

tourist guide

Villages, towns and cities

village

city

Places change

historic centre

new part

outskirts

Services in a city

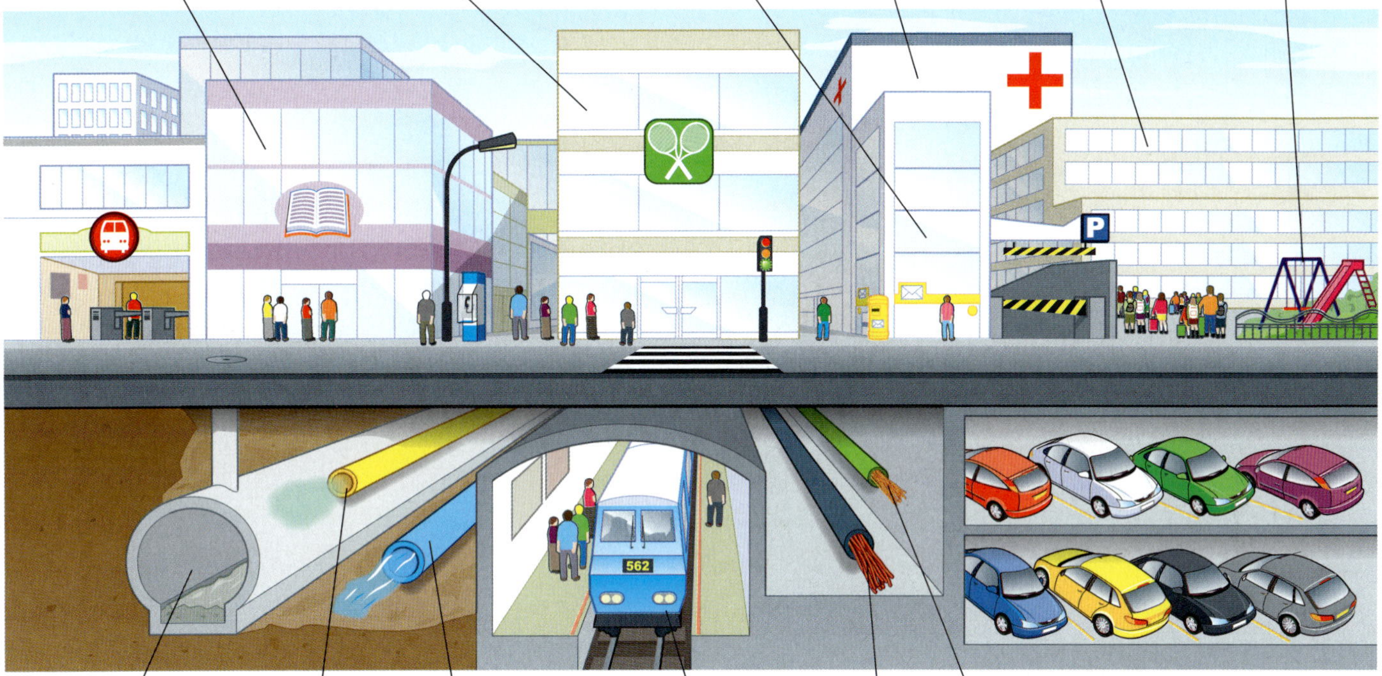

Finding your way around

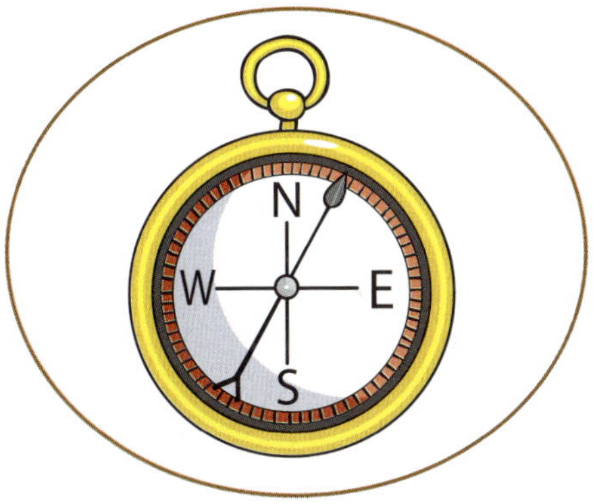

compass

GPS

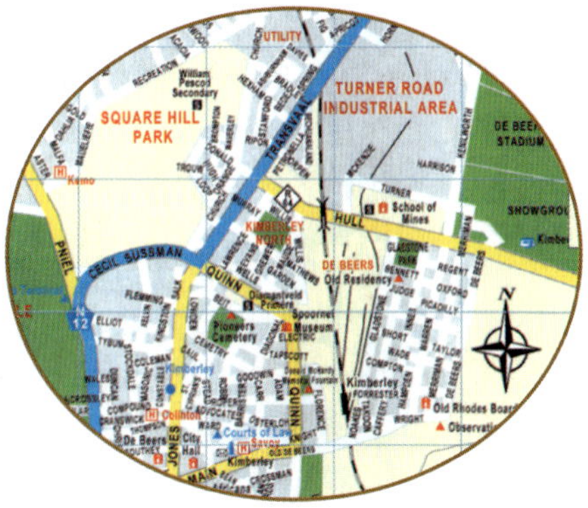

map

Macmillan Education
4 Crinan Street
London N1 9XW
A division of Springer Nature Limited
Companies and representatives throughout the world

ISBN 978 0 2307 2016 9

First published 2011

Written by Helen Sanderson
Designed by Anthony Godber
Illustrated by Ángeles Peinador, Mark Ruffle, Laszlo Veres, Ian Escott, Norbert Sipos, Anthony Rule, Kathy Baxendale and Oxford Designers and Illustrators
Cover design by Mark Slader
Cover illustration by Elmentcius Koronel
Course consultant: Rocío Gutiérrez Burgos
Science consultant: Graham Peacock
Picture research by Zoe Spilberg
Recordings produced by James Richardson
Songs composed and arranged by Mark Fishlock

Author's acknowledgements
I would like to thank the staff at Macmillan for being so helpful and such good advisors at all times throughout this project. I am also very grateful to my patient mother for her support and suggestions during the writing process and to my father for his advice on scientific matters. And finally a big thank you to my husband and children for making it possible for me to work on this very enjoyable project at home.

Acknowledgements
The author and publishers would like to thank the following teachers and schools: Almudena Ibeas Jiménez, Colegio. Nuestra Señora de las Nieves, Madrid; Aránzazu Sánchez Rodríguez, C.P. Rosa de Luxemburgo, Aravaca, Madrid; Carlos Pérez Guillén, C.E.I.P. Dionisio Ridruejo, Madrid; Carmen Marcos Salazar, C.E.I.P. Ciudad de Columbia, Tres Cantos, Madrid; Catherine M. Anner, Colegio Internacional Alminar, Dos Hermanas, Sevilla; Celia Ojeda Esnoz, Colegio Alameda de Osuna, Madrid; Dionisio Jesús Montoya Lozano, Colegio Saladares –Grupo Attendis–, Roquetas de Mar, Almería; Eduardo Obeso Ceballos, C.P. Rosa de Luxemburgo, Aravaca, Madrid; Eider Goikouría Basterretxea, Colegio Jesús María, Bilbao, Vizcaya; Esther Ninou Rodríguez, Escola Sant Gervasi, Mollet del Vallès, Barcelona; Estíbaliz Medina Martín, C.P. Virgen de Navalazarza, San Agustín de Guadalix, Madrid; Eva Ampuero López, C.E.I.P. Emilio Casado, Alcobendas, Madrid; Francisca García Fraile, C.E.I.P. Fontarrón, Madrid; Gema Mena Blasco, C.E.I.P. Infanta Elena, Pozuelo de Alarcón, Madrid; Jairo Dopazo Alonso, Colgeio Bilingüe Vallmont, Villanueva de la Cañada, Madrid; Janine Grant, Colegio Highlands, Sevilla; José Enrique Porras Ogalla, C.E.I.P. El Encinar, Torrelodones, Madrid; Laura Arroyo Campos, C.E.I.P. Ciudad de Columbia, Tres Cantos, Madrid; Laura Benítez Coloma, Institució La Miranda, Sant Just Desvern, Barcelona; María Cantó Collado, Colegio Bilingüe Vallmont, Villanueva de la Cañada, Madrid; Paloma González Megido, C.P. Marqués de Santillana, Palencia; Paula López Cabello, C.E.I.P. Gonzalo Fernández Córdoba, Madrid; Pilar Velasco García, C.P. Marqués de Santillana, Palencia; Roser Cantón Riera, Col·legi Marinada, Palau Solita i Plegamans, Barcelona; Sandra Rodríguez Figueroa, Colegio Internacional Alminar, Dos Hermanas, Sevilla; Sergio González Cenalmor, C.E.I.P. Vicente Aleixandre, Alcorcón, Madrid; Silvia San José Paul, C.E.I.P. El Cantizal, Las Rozas, Madrid; Susan Dreguer, Barcelona; Usoa García Hernández, Colegio Nuestra Señora de Europa, Getxo, Vizcaya; Zuriñe Sánchez, Colegio Sagrado Corazón Carmelitas, Vitoria-Gasteiz, Álava.

The publishers would like to thank Anthony Godber for his design expertise and invaluable input, Enric Custodio Fitó for his science expertise and advice, and Jessica Ocaña for her input and support.

Cover credit: Paul Bricknell

The authors and publishers would like to thank the following for permission to reproduce their photographic material:
Alamy/ Alchemy p55(bl), Alamy/ Amana Images Inc p37(background), Alamy/ Arco Images GmBH pp78(tr), 88(cr), 162(tr), Alamy/ Jennika Argent p130(tcr), Alamy/ Tom Bean pp75(r), 107(tr), 112(l), Alamy/ Blickwinkel pp47(d), 54(bl), 55(cr), 57(br), 64(c), 156(whale), Alamy/ Bon Appetit p109(cr), Alamy/ Mark Boulton p66(br), Alamy/ Paul Bourdice pp140(r), 172(bl), Alamy/ Mark Bretherton p57(cb), Alamy/ Paul Brough p69(c), Alamy/ John Cancalosi p48, Alamy/ Jim Cartwright pp118(r), 169(tr), Alamy/ Nigel Cattlin pp111(tl), 130(tl), Alamy/ David Taylor Photography pp95(br), 165(br), Alamy/ Adrian Davies p62, Alamy/ Daniel Dempster Photography p55(tl), Alamy/ E. R. Degginer p109(tr), Alamy/ Erin Paul Donovan p57(tl), Alamy/ John Eccles p71(bcl), Alamy/ Patrick Eden p93(bl), Alamy/ Brian Elliott pp45(g), 157(cb), Alamy/ Joe Fox pp114(br), 168(bl), Alamy/ Tim Gartside/ Travel South Africa pp78(br), 88(l), 162(br), Alamy/ Global Warming Images p67(tl), Alamy/ Glow Images p59(l), Alamy/ Chris Gomersall pp68(r), 160(tr), Alamy/ Juergen Hasenkopt p33(tr), Alamy/ Edward Herwick pp81(bl), 163(br), Alamy/ D. Hurst pp144, 173(c,), Alamy/ Ilian Animal p47(b), p47(d), Alamy/ Imagebroker pp78(tl), 87(tr), 88(cl), 129(l), 162(tl), Alamy/ Imagestate Media Partners Ltd – Impact Photos p131(ct), Alamy/ Jose Manuel Revuelta Luna pp115(tl, br), 68(train, metro), Alamy/ Juergen Henkelmann Photography pp139(t), 146(r), Alamy/ Kaien Kaku pp66(tr), 76(l), 160(cr), Alamy/ Christian Lagerek pp114(cl), 168(cb), Alamy/ Manor Photography pp10(br), 45(c, tr), 114(cr), 157(cr), 168(bike), Alamy/ Anette Mossbacker p66(bl), Alamy/ Motoring Picture Library pp114(tr), 148(ct), 168(tl), Alamy/ Dan O'Flynn pp43(cr), 156(bc), Alamy/ Alan Oliver p15(l), Alamy/ Tony Peacock pp140(bl), 172(bc), Alamy/ PhotoStock Israel p57(ct), Alamy/ Pictorium pp115(tr), 168(motorbike), Alamy/ Julie Pigula p59(r), Alamy/ SC Photos p52(b), Alamy/ Martin Shields pp11(b), 14(tr), 131(b), Alamy/ Linda Sneddon pp43(cl, 51(bcr), 156(bl), Alamy/ Christopher Taylor p45(a), Alamy/ Peter Titmuss pp133(cb), 171(br), Alamy/ Kirk Treakle p55(br), Alamy/ Tommy Tucker pp95(tl), 165(tl), Alamy/ Westend61 GmBH p61(euros), Alamy/ Wildlife GmbH p109(tl), Alamy/ Gordon Wood pp71(tr), 159(br); **Bananastock**/ pp8(tl), 9(l), 18(t), 25(bl), 126(tl), 171(tl); **Brand X**/ pp15(br), 45(d), 119(c), 151(cr), 157(tr); **Comstock**/ pp90(t inset), 92(tl inset); **Corbis**/ pp5(t), 10(cl), 14(ct), 25(tr), 47(c), 49(tr poster), 151(ct, cl, br), Corbis/ AlaskaStock pp72(cr), 160(bcr), Corbis/ Yann Arthus-Bertrand pp5(b), 92(tr), Corbis/ Atlandtide Phototravel pp78(cl), 162(cl), Corbis/ Blue Images p14(tl), Corbis/ Stewart Cohen/ Blend Images p9(c), Corbis/ Fridmar Damm pp107(b), 112(r), Corbis/ Odilon Dimier/ Photo Alto p33(bl), Corbis/ Kevin Dodge pp133(bl), Corbis/ Emely pp126(tr), 171(bl), Corbis/ Randy Faris p17(tl), Corbis/ Firefly Productions p33(d), Corbis/ Kevin Fleming pp129(r), Corbis/ Michael & Patricia Fogden p47(a), Corbis/ Frank and Helena/ Cultura pp81(tcr), 163(tcr), Corbis/ Willard Culver/ National Geographic Society pp127(tl), 136(l), 170(ct), Corbis/ Frank Lane Picture Agency/ B. Borrell Casals p55(tr), Corbis/ Stephen Frink pp40(cb), 50(c), Corbis/ Jose Fuste Raga p86, Corbis/ Gallo Images pp52(t), 157(tl), Corbis/ Kristy-Anne Glubish/ Design Pics pp25(br), 118(ct), 169(cr), Corbis/ Rick Gomez p18(b), Corbis/ Cat Gwynn p17(tr), Corbis/ Antoine Gyori/ Sygma p131(cb), Corbis/ Klaus Hackenberg pp72(l), 160(bl), Corbis/ Don Hammond/ Design Pics pp56, 158, Corbis/ Frithjof Hirdes pp81(tcl), 163(tcl), Corbis/ Corey Hochachka/ Design Pics pp95(bl), 165(bl), Corbis/ Fritz Hoffmann/ In Pictures pp126(bl), 136(c), 170(bc), Corbis/ Image Shop pp61(bc), 159(bl), Corbis/ Gerolf Kalt p71(tcl), Corbis/ Bert Klassen/ First Light pp54(br), 64(r), Corbis/ Bernd Kohlhas p63(l), Corbis/ Bear Lark p8(br), Corbis/ Ludovic Maisant pp107(c), 112(c), Corbis/ Lawrence Manning pp61(tl), 159(c), Corbis/ Jim Merli/ Visuals Unlimited p157(bl), Corbis/ Patrick Molnar p33(br), Corbis/ Tim Pannell p134, Corbis/ Ocean pp78(cr), 88(r), 162(cr), Corbis/ Steve Sparrow/ Cultura p84(tl), Corbis/ Stuart O'Sullivan p52(ct), Corbis/ Robert Pickett pp71(bcr), 111(tr), Corbis/ Michael Pole p105, Corbis/ Hans Reinhard p71(br), Corbis/ Denis Scott p74, Corbis/ Liba Taylor p84(bl), Corbis/ Gabriel Tizon p135, Corbis/ Visuals Unlimited p109(cl), Corbis/ Gaby Wojciech/ Westend 61 pp61(c), 159(bcl), Corbis/ Pawel Wysocki/ Hemis pp66(tl), 76(r), 100(ct), 160(tl), Corbis/ Elisabet

Zeilon/ Etsa pp130(tr), Corbis/ Jim Zuckerman pp69(l), 75(l), 160(ct); **Creatas**/ pp47(f), 151(c); **Digital Stock**/ pp10(tl), 41(ct), 42(cr), 156(butterfly); **Digital Vision**/ pp40(tr), 50(cr), 41(tl), 42(bl), 43(l), 51(tcl), 99(cr), 115(cl), 156(tl, tr), 168(ferry); **Eyewire**/ p49(poster); **Fotolibra**/ Peter Curno p91, Fotolibra/ Xavier Fores, Joana Roncero pp138, 146(l), Fotolibra/ Maria Galan pp115(cr), 168(ct), 172(cr), Fotolibra/ Nikhilesh Haval pp119(l), 169(br); **Getty**/ pp97(l), 99(br), 114(tl), 120(c), 145(cb), 168(tr), Getty/ Christian Adams p92(tl), Getty/ Susan Barr p34, Getty/ Karen Bentham p87(b), Getty/ Michael Blann pp127(ct), 132, 170(br), Getty/ Paul Burns pp127(tr), 170(bl), Getty/ Julien Capmeil pp67(tr), 160(cl), Getty/ De Agostini Picture Library pp45(br), 93(tl), Getty/ Robert Daly p52(cb), Getty/ Steve Dunwell p33(c), Getty/ Tim Flach p130(tcl), Getty/ Sonja Grunbauer p117(ctr), Getty/ Image Source pp133(br), 136(r), 171(tcl), Getty/ Jupiter Images pp36, 117(br), Getty/ Kallista Images p33(b), Getty/ Dave King p63(r), Getty/ Jens Kuhfs pp41(cb), 51(bl), 156(crab), Getty/ James Lauritz pp114(bl), 168(br), Getty/ David Oldfield p17(cr), Getty/ Siede Preis pp61(tr), 159(bc), Getty/ Joseph Sohm/ Visions of America p97(r), Getty/ u3k-y p69(r); **Grapheast**/ p151(bl); **Image Source**/ pp22(bl), 84(br), 90(b inset), 91(inset), 93(b inset), 97(inset); **IT Stock**/ p15(tr); **John Foxx Images**/ pp40(tl), 50(l), 156(ct); **Jupiter Images**/ p151(tl); **Macmillan Publishers Ltd**/ pp8(tr), 145(bl, tr), Macmillan Publishers Australia Ltd/ pp8(bl, ct), 14(cr), 40(br), 50(r), 51(br, tl), 151(cb), Macmillan Publishers Ltd/ Haddon Davies p61(cr, tcr), Macmillan Publishers New Zealand Ltd/ p87(tl), Macmillan Publishers South Africa Ltd/ p173(r); **Nature Picture Library**/ Terry Andrewartha pp45(bl), 157(br), Nature Picture Library/ Nigel Bean pp42(tr), 47(e), Nature Picture Library/ Niall Benvie pp42(br), 156(toad), Nature Picture Library/ Jane Burton p45(f), Nature Picture Library/ Philippe Clement pp41(tr), 156(br), Nature Picture Library/ Suzi Eszterhas p67(bl), Nature Picture Library/ Duncan McEwan p44, Nature Picture Library/ Gary K Smith pp10(cr), 14(cl), Nature Picture Library/ Carol Walker p45(b), Nature Picture Library/ Doug Wechsler p71(tcr); **NHPA**/ Oceans-Image/ Photshot pp43(r), 156(lobster); **Photoalto**/ p14(bl); **Photodisc**/ pp8(cb), 10(bl), 12, 40(bl), 41(bl, br), 50(cl), 51(tcr, tr), 99(bl, cb), 145(br), 157(ct); **Photolibrary**/ Age fotostock pp33(e, f), 84(tr), 90(b), Photolibrary/ Gonzalo Azumendi p172(tl), Photolibrary/ Barbara Boensch p117(bl), Photolibrary/ Brand X p122, Photolibrary/ BSIP Medical p25(tl), Photolibrary/ ComStock pp133(tl), Photolibrary/ Gary Conner pp133(ct), 171(cb), Photolibrary/ Creatas pp81(br), 163(br), Photolibrary/ Jeff Dunn p67(br), Photolibrary/ Euroluftbildde pp93(br), 102(b), Photolibrary/ Ron Evans p59(c), Photolibrary/ F1 Online p156(lizard), Photolibrary/ Jules Frazier pp61(br), 159(tr), Photolibrary/ Yashuhide Fumoto pp119(cr), 169(bl), Photolibrary/ Garden Picture Library p71(tl), Photolibrary/ Glow Images p17(br), Photolibrary/ Laurent Grandadam pp133(tr), 171(cr), Photolibrary/ Gerald Hoberman p98, Photolibrary/ Reinhard Holzl pp54(tr), 57(bl), Photolibrary/ Image 100 pp95(tr), 165(tr), Photolibrary/ Ingram Publishing pp78(bl), 81(tl), 102(cb), 162(bl), 163(tl), Photolibrary/ Inti St Clair pp127(bl), 171(tr), Photolibrary/ Jonathan Kitchen p58, Photolibrary/ G & R Maschmeyer p131(t), Photolibrary/ Jerry & Marcy Monkman p93(tr), Photolibrary/ Jose Antonio Moreno p139(b), Photolibrary/ Nacho Moro pp140(tl), 148(b), 172(br), Photolibrary/ Clive Nichols pp54(tl), 64(l), 102(t), Photolibrary/ Pixland p13, Photolibrary/ Tony Robins pp61(bl), 159(tl), Photolibrary/ Rubberball p17(cb), Photolibrary/ Stockbrokerxtra Images p57(tr), Photolibrary/ Bjorn Svensson pp127(br), 148(cb), 170(tr), Photolibrary/ The Travel Library Ltd p90(t), Photolibrary/ David Tipling pp72(cl), 111(br), 160(bcl), Photolibrary/ Guenter Wamser pp61(cl), 159(bcr), Photolibrary/ Holger Winkler p151(tr); **Pixtal**/ p14(c); **Powerstock**/ p41(tl); **Rex Features**/ p120(l), Rex Features/ F1 Online pp115(bl), 117(tr), 168(helicopter), Rex Features/ Michael S. Nolan/ Splashdown Direct pp68(l), 160(c), Rex Features/ Pekka Sakki p22(bcl), Rex Features/ Sipa Press pp110, 117(bcr), Rex Features/ Voisin/ Phanie pp126(br), 170(tl), Rex Features/ Greg Watts p71(bl), Rex Features/ R. G. Williamson p117(tl), Rex Features/ Alf Wilson pp81(tr), 163(tr); **Science Photo Library**/ Joyce Photographics p109(bl), Science Photo Library/ D. Roberts p33(a), Science Photo Library/ Kaj R. Svensson p109(br), Science Photo Library/ Steve Vowles pp72(r), 160(br), Science Photo Library/ Jeanne White p51(bcl); **Still Pictures**/ Biosphoto/ Cordier Sylvain pp45(c), 157(cl); **Stockbyte**/ pp24, 99(tr), 111(bl), 145(tl); **Superstock**/ Glow Images Cuisine p9(r).

Commissioned photography by Paul Bricknell: pp 9(laptop),11, 14, 19, 20, 21, 22(boy, fingerprints), 23, 31, 32, 37(diary, glue stick, pencil), 41(laptop), 49(girl, corkboard), 61(b), 69(laptop), 73, 80, 83, 94(a-d), 95(laptop), 96(laptop), 99(boy, corkboard), 105(boy), 106(girl), 116(girl), 118(mobile, postcard), 119(magazine, newspaper), 120,128, 133(laptop), 142(laptop), 143(a-d), 145(girl, corkboard), 148(t), 159(paper)169(mobile, postcard, magazine, newspaper).
My Science Project pages(scissors, pencil, glue stick) pp 63, 75, 87, 111, 123, 135.

Thanks to Bobby, Gloria & Josephine.

Printed and bound in Spain by Edelvives

2022 2021 2020 2019 2018
25 24 23 22 21 20 19